CARO

ON

GAMBLING

By
Mike Caro
"The Mad Genius"

A GAMBLING TIMES BOOK

DISTRIBUTED BY
LYLE STUART
Secaucus, N.J.

CARO ON GAMBLING

Copyright © 1984 by Gambling Times Incorporated

CARO, MIKE
CARO ON GAMBLING

ISBN: 0-89746-029-4

Distributed by Lyle Stuart, Inc.

Manufactured in the United States of America
Printed and Bound by Kingsport Press
(First Printing — January 1984)

Editor: *Eleanor M. Saris*
Cover Design: *Terry Robinson*
Cover Illustration: *Laurie Newell*

All material presented in this book is offered as information to the reader. No inducement to gamble is intended or implied.

Other *Gambling Times* Books Available—Current Releases

(See page 178 for details.)

Poker Books

According to Doyle
by Doyle Brunson
Caro's Book of Tells by Mike Caro
The GT Official Rules of Poker
by Mike Caro
Poker For Women by Mike Caro
Poker Without Cards by Mike Caro
Wins, Places and Pros
by Tex Sheahan

Blackjack Books

The Beginner's Guide to Winning
Blackjack by Stanley Roberts
The GT Guide to Blackjack
by Stanley Roberts and others
Million Dollar Blackjack
by Ken Uston

Casino Games

The GT Guide to Casino Games
by Len Miller
The GT Guide to Craps
by N.B. Winkless, Jr.

General Interest Books

According to GT: The Rules of
Gambling Games
by Stanley Roberts

The GT Guide to Gaming Around
the World
The GT Guide to Systems That
Win, Volumes I and II
The GT Guide to Winning
Systems, Volumes I and II
GT Presents Winning Systems and
Methods, Volumes I and II
The Mathematics of Gambling
by Dr. Edward O. Thorp
Odds: Quick and Simple
by Mike Caro
P$yching Out Vegas
by Marvin Karlins, Ph.D.
Winning By Computer
by Dr. Donald Sullivan

Sports Betting Books

The GT Guide to Basketball
Handicapping by Barbara Nathan
The GT Guide to Football
Handicapping by Bob McCune
The GT Guide to Greyhound
Racing by William E. McBride
The GT Guide to Harness Racing
by Igor Kusyshyn, Ph.D.,
Al Stanley and Sam Dragich
The GT Guide to Jai Alai
by William R. Keevers
The GT Guide to Thoroughbred
Racing by R.G. Denis

The following *Gambling Times* books
are scheduled for release in September 1984:

Poker Books

Caro's Poker Encyclopedia
by Mike Caro

**Free Money: How to Win in the
Cardrooms of California**
by Michael Wiesenberg

The Railbird by Rex Jones

Tales Out of Tulsa
by Bobby Baldwin

**World Class Poker, Play by
Play** by Mike Caro

General Interest Books

Caro On Computer Gambling
by Mike Caro

The GT Quiz Book
by Mike Caro

How the Superstars Gamble
by Ron Delpit

**How to Win at Gaming
Tournaments** by Haven Earle Haley

**You're Comped: How to Be a
Casino Guest** by Len Miller

Sports Betting Books

**Fast Track to
Harness Racing Profits**
by Mark Cramer

**Fast Track to
Thoroughbred Profits**
by Mark Cramer

FOREWORD

For five years Mike Caro has clarified and pioneered some of the most important gambling concepts ever put on paper. He is consultant to many of the world's leading poker players and his advice on casino games and gambling in general is highly regarded throughout the world.

Caro is primarily known as a teacher and theorist, but beyond that — twice world poker champion, Doyle Brunson, calls him "the best draw poker player alive."

His in-depth statistics on poker and gambling are among the most widely quoted today. Caro is a computer wizard who uses his exclusive programs to back up his research. In addition, he is famous for his work on the psychology and philosophy of gambling. In fact, his new book, *CARO'S BOOK OF TELLS (The Body Language of Poker),* promises to rank among the most popular gambling literature of all time.

In 1983 Caro gave a paid seminar at Palace Station in Las Vegas and drew 158 people, many traveling from out of state to hear his two-hour lecture on poker. At full-scale gambling-related seminars, he draws audiences who pay as much as $195.

Caro is known as *"The Mad Genius,"* and for good reason. Much of his teaching is unconventional and very profound. Yet he explains things in crisp, clear language that will have your pulse racing as you learn the secret keys to winning.

This book is mostly a prized collection of the column "CARO ON GAMBLING" — a regular monthly feature in *Gambling Times* magazine. A few segments are taken from Caro's column, "A Word From the Mad Genius," running in the *Poker Player* newspaper of which he is Editor-in-Chief.

We think what you're about to read will surprise you. And if gambling is part of your nature, this book might become your best friend for life.

THE PUBLISHER

Illustration by Stan Hunt

Mike Caro as "Crazy Mike" when
everyone expected bizarre behavior...

..............................today Caro is a little tamer and is famous as "The Mad Genius." He's seen here rehearsing for the Poker Seminar at the Stardust Hotel and Casino in Las Vegas.

TABLE OF CONTENTS

PART ONE

Some Basic Truths About Gambling

"Adventurers tend to prance about the
ladder of success, fearing less the
sensation of a great fall than the
humility of hanging idle."

Chapter 1

Plodders vs. Adventurers

I hate money management. But wait! That's no way to begin a book on scientific gambling. After all, experts agree that money management is vital to a stable and secure bankroll. Sorry, I just blurted it out before I could stop myself, and now it's too late to take it back.

At least let me assure you that, in the pages ahead, we're going to tackle some really important stuff.

Fine. But, read the opening line again. Doesn't that strike you as a wildly irresponsible statement, coming from a presumed authority on poker tactics and probability?

Okay. Let me explain. Maybe you remember seeing posters in your high school hallways that read, "Sex!" and then in smaller print, "Now that we've got your attention, don't forget to tell your parents about the P.T.A. meeting this Friday..." That's advertising technique tested and proven. Start off with something to win their attention. Next, bombard them with the *real* message.

But isn't that a dirty trick, far beneath the dignity of this book? Good question. Anyway, now that all the ploys have been played, now that all the advertising techniques have been tried, now that we've gotten all the fun and frivolity out of the way, what's the real subject of this chapter?

I already told you — Money Management — I hate it!

I can't even stand the way it's spelled. Why should a fifteen-letter term waste 40% of itself on M's and N's? But that's just a minor grievance.

What really makes me mad is the way advocates of Double M go around preaching. They rely heavily on an almost spiritual concept called "stop loss" to protect them. They'll admonish you to risk only a specified percentage of your bankroll each day. To risk less is acceptable, but to risk more is grave transgression. Not content simply to claim that this magic maximum percentage was whispered by a prophet in the men's room, they argue that mathematicians have *proven* that theirs is the most profitable long-range approach for us all.

I'd like to respectfully point out the stupidity of this advice.

First. One valid reason to apply a stop loss is to prevent yourself from losing more than you're psychologically able to handle. Another is to safeguard yourself from devastating losses in situations where you may have miscalculated your profit potential. Conversely, it would be inexcusable to use a stop loss in a poker game where you *know* your hourly expectancy is $50, you feel alert, you want to play and you can emotionally tolerate a big loss. If under those circumstances, you quit three hours early because you've reached a pre-established loss limit, the average cost is $150.

Second. There *is* no maximum mathematically correct percentage of your bankroll you should be willing to risk on a given day. The more you wager relative to the size of your bankroll, the better your chances are of achieving sudden riches, and the more likely you are to go broke in the attempt. When you risk less, you're more secure, but you can't win as much. So there you have it, the simple truth. The amount of money you should bet is not governed by any universal formula. It is determined by *you,* your spirit, your courage, how much you value security and how well you can tolerate the pain of losing.

There seem to exist two main categories of professional gamblers. Those who plod along securely, accumulating their bankrolls methodically, and those who treat gambling as an adventure. Both groups have mastered techniques which afford them a winning edge.

The *plodders* prize security above all else. For them I recommend a solid system of money management.

The *adventurers* are willing to risk great agony in the pursuit of giant rewards. They tend to prance about the ladder of success, fearing less the sensation of a great fall than the humility of hanging idle. Here are the heroes in Western movies, ready to wager the ranch on the turn of a card.

Let's be honest. You and I both admire the adventurers more than the plodders. Just about every world class poker player I've ever known is an adventurer. Occasionally they may mumble something about money management but they don't use it very effectively. It goes against their nature. They're too daring, too courageous and, maybe, too reckless. Sure, sometimes they go broke, but not very often, and they can handle the pain when it happens.

Imagine a no-limit, heads-up poker contest between a plodder and an adventurer. Let's say they both have equal technical skills. Want a word of advice? Don't bet on the plodder. He has no heart.

4

Usually, plodders won't play against strong opposition, anyway. Challenge them and you're apt to hear, "There's a hundred soft spots around town. Why should I play against *you?*"Adventurers don't think that way. You'll see two world champions, Doyle Brunson and Bobby Baldwin — the best of friends away from the table — battling head-to-head for big stakes. Why? Simple. That's how you get to be the best. You can't be a great prizefighter by beating up kids on the playground. Sooner or later you've got to fight a guy who's likely to smash your face in. Adventurers welcome the opportunity to meet tough opponents. Plodders run and hide.

So thoroughly have plodders saturated gambling literature with their Double M fetish that a carefree gambler can't risk much of his bankroll without feeling guilty.

If you ever find yourself churning in misery after a terrible loss, you have a friend. You'll get no lectures here, only sympathy. If you're an adventurer, come out of hiding. Spread the word: The tyranny of Double M is over. Michael John Caro thinks you're a hero!

Chapter 2

The God of Irony Doesn't Gamble

The weirdest things happen to gamblers.

Last Tuesday I journeyed to Los Alamitos to watch the quarter-horse races. Although I'm not a regular horse player, I sometimes follow the advice of handicappers I respect.

Martin — brilliant, young Martin — is the sort of guy who is wholly devoted to horse racing. He studies the *Form* ritually from 7 a.m. till noon each day. For the past two years, he's earned a small profit, although you wonder if it's worth the effort. He certainly isn't getting rich, but at least he can truthfully say he's winning.

Martin's wife Laura — young, sexy Laura — shows no apparent fascination with his tireless evaluation of racing data. You get the idea she'd just as soon he cleared the kitchen table of all the *Forms*, calculators, pencils and scratch pads.

Nonetheless, she offered a smile when she opened the door to greet me. "Martin's almost ready. I'm going with you. I've never been to the track before."

"Really," I said.

"You guys and your *systems!* Well, I've got my own method," she explained. "I close my eyes and the winning horse comes to me. I know you think it's silly, but it works. At least it works on paper."

I couldn't tell whether she was serious, half-serious or joking. So I selected a tactical reply. "Sounds interesting."

Her six-year-old son Jasper — spoiled, noisy Jasper — ran up and glared at me defiantly. "I don't get to go to the races," he complained as if it were my fault. "I gotta stay here with the dumb babysitter. I *hate* horses."

When we arrived at the track, Martin decided that although he'd been flirting with a first-race bet it was better just to sit out this maiden event.

Laura, though, had her own ideas. She closed her eyes tight and rubbed them with her fingertips. She had just read the daily program and apparently the names of horses were racing through her nimble brain.

Finally she came up with one. It was, *"Pass Em Twice.* I really feel good about that horse."

"Don't forget your five-dollar limit," Martin reminded as his wife dashed merrily toward the ticket window.

Turning to me, he said, "I made her promise not to bet over five bucks a race. Good thing, too. I do my handicapping in reverse order, crossing off horses that don't stand a chance first. *Pass Em Twice* was the first one I eliminated. But let her have her fun."

Laura had fun. The horse paid $47.20!

"Was that a good horse or was I just lucky?" Laura asked her husband impetuously.

"Good horse," he snarled — lovingly.

Martin had a key pick going in the second. It was *Go Oh Tory.*

"Mine starts with an 'F'," said Laura, once again pressing her eyes and trying to visualize the name. It's either *Front Page Star* or *Famous Sir. Famous Sir,* that's the one."

It paid $10.40. *Go Oh Tory* ran third.

I know what you're thinking. This is beginning to sound like one of those silly movies where the woman always wins at the expense of the male ego. But I'm keeping as close to the truth as I know how.

Already Martin was suffering some minor humiliation.

The winners of the next three races were *Limited Policy* (paying $10.80), *Splash A Rocket* ($22.40) and *Sir Dancelot* ($8.60). Laura picked them all. She was having fun, all right! Following Martin's learned advice, we bet three horses that finished out of the money. In fairness, I'll point out that he *almost* chose *Sir Dancelot* in the fifth, but opted instead for *Plenty of Nothing.*

"How can you bet a horse called *Plenty of Nothing,*" Laura chided prior to the race. "It gives me shivers just thinking about it."

By this time, Laura (who had bet exactly $5 each race) was winning over $200. Martin and I sported a combined loss of nearly $2000, the bulk of it his.

Next he picked *Asyouare.* When Laura finally opened her eyes after minutes of meditation, she announced her choice, *"Asyouare."*

Martin and I laughed. "This has got to be a good omen," he decided. We emptied out on the sixth race, betting everything left in our pockets, including $5 for Laura. *Asyouare* didn't win.

As we were leaving the parking lot, Laura kissed her husband tenderly on the cheek. "I'm sorry you had such a bad time, honey. But don't you think I did pretty good, winning five out of six races?"

"You know, I had a *feeling* that was going to happen," Martin confided later. "It was a strong premonition. I just said to myself, 'Here I've been trying to impress Laura how important it is to gamble scientifically. What's the worst thing that could happen?' I tell you, Mike, it's like I dreamed up the whole nightmare and then *made* it happen."

A couple of years ago I would have dismissed Martin's complaint as purely ludicrous. Of late I'm beginning to wonder...

Last year I was playing in a $40-limit game with a friend, Ernie Wilson. We were both losing, so we decided to "low spade" for $100 a hand. The rules of that game were simple: every time a poker hand is dealt, whichever of us held the lowest spade won $100. No skill involved. For convenience, I kept score on paper with the understanding that payment would be made whenever one of us quit.

I'd been running particularly bad on this gamble for years, so I teased, "You shouldn't have any problem with me, Ernie. I haven't studied *this* game."

I got off immediately to a 7-1 lead, meaning Ernie was stuck $600. "I think I'm mastering the strategy," I gloated, knowing well that this was merely a 50-50 proposition.

By the time we reached the 69th decision, I had a 47-22 lead! Now I was apologizing sincerely, because it just didn't seem fair. If you have even a vague mathematical intuition, you realize how remarkable this kind of lopsided result is.

"I can't understand it," I said, "I never beat anyone at this game. Hang in there, Ernie. Things tend to even out."

I really didn't mean it, of course. Secretly, I was happy about this $2500 windfall which was getting me close to even for the night. But then, as I said the words, "Things will even out," I had this dark premonition about all the luck flowing back to Ernie.

About an hour later we were tied 56-56, and we called off the gamble. He had outscored me 34-9 during that run! Some of you probability purists may recognize just how bizarre this is.

Sure, it could have been just a freak natural occurrence, but so many things like this happen in the lives of gamblers that sometimes we wonder. Don't we?

I made Ernie sign a statement that this had actually transpired, in the presence of Richard Richards, another top-calibre draw player. We'll call that statement Exhibit A.

Exhibit B is an event about eight months old.

A middle-aged man was sitting at a lowball game right across the table from me. He was losing roughly $500 and seemed irritated. Then his wife approached from a small-limit game and demanded $20.

"Did you lose your fifty bucks already?" the man hissed.

"I just got three pat sevens in a row and they all lost. What am I supposed to do," she fired back.

He handed her the $20 in chips angrily waving her away. "You never even *got* three pat sevens in a row in your life!" he snarled. "Nobody *ever lost* on three pat sevens in a row! Don't make things sound worse than they are!"

The woman walked away swearing to herself, severely embarrassed.

Of course, the man was right in speculating his wife was lying. Using the 53-card joker-added deck, standard in California, the odds against even being dealt three pat sevens on three specified hands are 2,751,140-1. When you consider that in a typical game these will stand up 75% of the time, the odds against what the woman claimed are 176,073,014-1. Of course, everyone gets a pat seven beat now and then, so if you use *that* as your starting point, the odds against getting two more mutilated aren't nearly as great.

But, anyway, here's the good part. The man, still irritated because of his wife's intrusion, got in a raising war with me. I had a pat six. His was a pat 7-6-4-3-2.

Leaving his cards face-up on the table, he stood up angrily and bellowed to his wife. She hurried back to the table.

"See!" he shouted, "That's a *real* seven that just got cracked!"

The next hand he had a pat 7-5-4-3-A which lost to a two-card bicycle!

Everyone else at the table had to be thinking the same thing I was: *Wouldn't it be ironic if it happened for the third time in a row!*

Well, it did! This time he was dealt 7-6-5-2-joker. He collided with a one-card 7-4-3-2-A!

Taking his few remaining chips with him, he stormed from the club, his wife chasing behind him.

I've seen a lot of dramatic coincidences happen to gamblers. Without specifying, we'll call them Exhibits C through Y.

Now we come to Exhibit Z, the straw that scratched the camel's back (or however the saying goes).

Last night I was playing draw poker and a player rushed to the table from nowhere. "Hey, M.J.C., what are the odds against getting a pat bicycle?"

i told him they were 1,245-1. Then I promptly picked up my hand. You guessed it, 5-4-3-2-A. The odd thing about it was that after looking at only the ace I *felt* it coming. Now Exhibit Z really isn't remarkable in itself, but it was the catalyst for this chapter.

Everyone I've talked to in depth about gambling confesses the same secret feelings. This even includes mathematicians who think something strange might be happening in the universe.

Well, I know what it is!

Yep, after years and years of pondering the inexplicable, I've stumbled upon an answer. There's a reason why gamblers always complain of witnessing the "most incredible thing" or events that are simply "unbelievable."

I have isolated and identified the God of Irony! He alone is responsible for all those "impossible" bad beats. It's his only job and he does it tirelessly. Worst of all he doesn't gamble.

Let me tell you something about the God of Irony so you know what you're up against. This is the guy who waits for you to begin a thought with the words "Wouldn't it be terrible if. . ." or "Can you imagine how bad I'd feel after winning all this money if. . ."

You think those thoughts and you're apt to gain the attention of the God of Irony. The most dangerous thoughts are ones like, "The only way I could possibly lose this game is if we fumble the ball and the other guys get off a 90-yard touchdown drive in 54 seconds."

You think that and you're in trouble! I mean, am I right or *am I right?* You've had things like that happen to you a hundred times, haven't you?

Let's say the odds are 200-1 in your favor. Then a dark, desperate idea crosses your mind. You find yourself envisioning a way to lose. The minute the idea strikes you, you're only a 5-1 favorite. That's because there's a good chance the God of Irony will have intercepted your idea and decided to use it.

It can happen on the golf course when you're gambling for big bucks. You're leading by a stroke on the 18th and your opponent has just chipped a shot that's going to roll 50 feet past the hole.

You're practically spending your money, but then this thought hits you. "I've lost six weeks in a row to this bastard. Everything's gone wrong. Wouldn't it be ironic if that ball hit the pin and dropped in for a birdie!"

Enter the God of Irony. Ping! Plunk! You lose.

Hey, you gamblers know what I'm talking about, don't you? The craziest things happen to us all the time.

Truth is, the God of Irony is a pretty dull fellow. He never has a creative thought of his own. We keep putting stuff in his head. The little sucker knows a good idea when he hears it.

Now, maybe you think I'm being facetious. Is this just mental medicine to help you ease the pain of losing?

Many gamblers think they've been singled out by fate as a target for cruel jokes. They feel they alone in all the universe are being tortured, experimented upon by some unknown force. They scream and cry deep within themselves. The hurt goes on.

I think it's better to believe in the God of Irony. At least you know who the enemy is — a pathetic little being with too much power and not a single worthwhile idea of his own.

So, let's stop feeling miserable when things go bad and start exchanging God of Irony stories.

But if you refuse to believe that there is such a beast, go on thinking those strange thoughts. And when you finally get that pat full house you've been waiting for all week and your mind blurts, "Wouldn't it be terrible if this lost!" Don't say I didn't warn you!

PART TWO

Deeper Truth

"People gamble to get it over with."

Chapter 3

In Search of the Right Winning Attitude

Pretend I'm dead. The autopsy shows no evidence of alcohol or drugs. No foul play is suspected. You approach my body, inspired by a mysterious smile frozen on my lips. Is it a trick? You watch for subtle movement; you listen for some sign of shallow breathing.

Finally, you shake your head dismally. "I guess Mike Caro isn't bluffing," you whisper to yourself. Maybe it's a case of poker fatigue, but who cares? Dead is dead.

Please use all your best powers of imagination. It is very important that this vision appears real. Still not convinced? You study me for a very long time, but there is no indication of life. No faint flutter of an eyelid.

Suddenly I speak. Immediately you know damn well you're going to listen and obey. The first thing that flashes to mind is that old saying: *Dead men don't tell lies*. But like many folk sayings, this one has crumbled under recent scientific investigation. It turns out that some dead men *do* tell lies. In particular, dead politicians lie. Dead fishermen lie. Even dead preachers lie. But you're aware of another recent scientific finding: *Dead gamblers never lie*.

That's why you're prepared to accept anything I say without argument. I'm glad, because if you were just reading the following ideas anywhere else, you'd consider them opinion. This way you're going to know they're the truth and you'll obey and profit.

So keep imagining.

The voice that comes from me is powerful and authoritative. It seeps from everywhere although my smile doesn't budge. Clearly this is not a voice emanating normally.

My first words are: "Why do you gamble?"

Please choose your response from the following list:

(1) I gamble for the challenge.

(2) I gamble because I'm bored.

(3) I gamble to win money.

(4) I gamble to lose money.
(5) I gamble to be social.
(6) I gamble for the excitement.
(7) I gamble because it makes me happy.
(8) I gamble because I'm sick.
(9) I gamble because nobody cares.

When you've given me your answer, I respond, "That's pretty good. Actually, I was prepared to accept any answer you offered. You see, gambling needs no justification. If I'd asked you why you drink water, you might have said, 'Because I'm thirsty' or 'To stay alive' or 'I'm trying to get wet.' Whatever you said would have been fine with me, because you can always *supply* a reason although you never *need* one."

You think about this for a few seconds. Although the truth looks a little vague, you are very sure these words will prove helpful. After all, they were uttered by a dead gambler.

I continue, "Instead of the answer you gave me, you should have said, *'I gamble to get it over with.'* Now there's a powerful truth! Everyone gambles to get it over with! That's the secret. No matter what causes you to gamble — a will to win, a will to lose, the need for excitement — your true hidden motivation is always to get it over with. You must understand that."

"This is beginning to make sense," you say politely, although you're not quite certain.

"Everyone is a compulsive gambler. Being a compulsive gambler is no worse and no better than being a compulsive breather. It is *everyone's* nature to gamble. Don't confuse being a compulsive gambler with being a compulsive loser. All the greatest professional gamblers have sooner or later decided to come to terms with their true natures."

"But I know a lot of people who hate to gamble," you object.

"They may have contempt for formalized games of chance, but they *do* gamble," I assert. Your spine tingles because you're hearing the wisdom of the dead. "And even though they may think they hate taking chances, they all do it.

"Everyone reaches out for risk. Everyone craves it. Some people may unconsciously seek out dangerous personal relationships. Rather than settle on a stable romance, they create an explosive situation in which they stalk a difficult reward while risking great pain. They are gamblers in the act of gambling.

"Every conscious act requires risk. Every conscious act requires decision. You put those two facts together and you realize that the secret to success in life is not to avoid gambling, but to gamble well."

After another hour, you're totally convinced of these truths:

(1) Every human being ever born was a compulsive gambler.

(2) Some gamblers compulsively win and some gamblers compulsively lose. Others compulsively don't care.

(3) Humans who fear formal games of chance tend to trick themselves into gambling more heavily in their daily interactions.

(4) Your success in life is dynamically connected to the quality of your gambling decisions.

(5) People who realize they are gambling have a much better chance of winning than people who deny that they gamble.

(6) As a group, the world's most reckless gamblers win life's biggest pots and share life's greatest miseries.

Some of these points you understood and some seemed obscure. Nonetheless, because these ideas all came from a dead gambler, you were glad you listened.

Finally, imagine that I left you with one command before my voice fell silent: "For one month, I want you to write a report at the end of each day. In a left-hand column, list the six most important events that happened to you personally today. Then, starting at the top of the list, fill in a second column which briefly describes how that event related to gambling. To the right of that, mark whether the main decisions you made were 'Conscious' or 'Unconscious.'

"Then, in the right most column, mark 'Good Gamble,' or 'Bad Gamble.'

"By the end of the month, you will have regained permanent and critical control of your life. In everyday activity, in the casinos and at the poker tables, you will make winning decisions. Although you will still gamble *to get it over with,* your objective will always be profit. You will be your own best fan and your own greatest coach. Trust me; I'm dead."

Chapter 4

Caro's Conception

Wanna share a secret?

Look, I'm not talking about some shallow and simplistic secret that flutters out of a fortune cookie. This is a vast and monumental secret. Even at its most superficial level, it will teach you a nifty proposition that's worth a lot of money. Think deeper, and you'll understand it at a higher level. Here you'll be able to save a *great deal* of money by avoiding sudden pitfalls and invisible peril. There's an even higher level of comprehension, one that will provide you with greater insight into the nature of life itself.

So what does it take to learn this secret? Not much. You only need to play an imaginary game, and the game goes like this. . .

You are alone at a poker table, sipping coffee and hoping for some players to show up. Can you picture it? That's right, there you are just minding your own business. Pretend that I take a seat across the table from you.

I say, "I'll bet you a hundred bucks on a proposition I just invented."

Now imagine that you reply, "Okay, it's a bet. Here's the hundred."

I know, you wouldn't say that because it would sound sort of stupid, not knowing what the proposition is. Well, pretend anyway. Why should you? Because otherwise you can't finish the game and you won't get to learn the secret.

Where were we? I remember — you say, "Here's the hundred."

"And here's the proposition," I begin, snatching the bill eagerly from your hand. Make believe that I now unfold a large poster and spread it across the table. Pasted on the poster are 27 poker hands arranged in three vertical columns — as shown in Figure 1, but don't look yet. "We each choose a column, then we play. We'll use some random method to select one hand from each of our columns. Since we can't draw cards, the best poker hand wins."

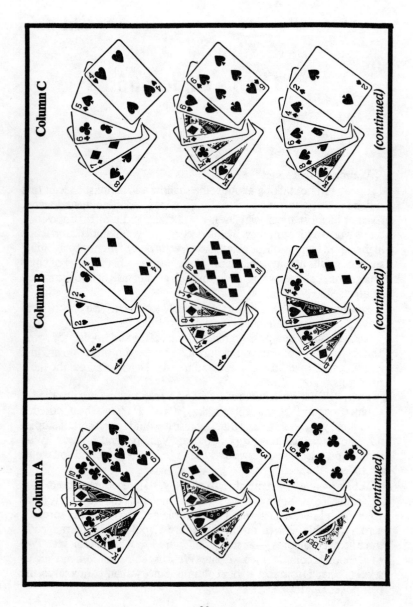

Column A

Column B

Column C

(continued)

(continued)

(continued)

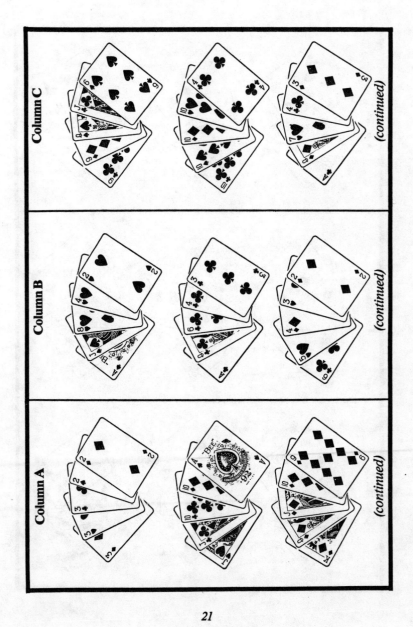

Column A   Column B   Column C

(continued)   *(continued)*   *(continued)*

21

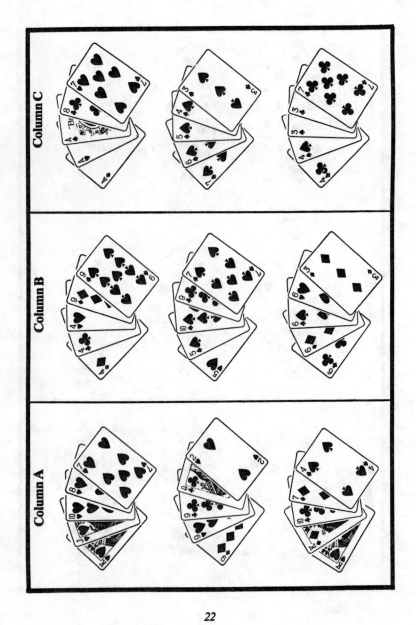

Column A   Column B   Column C

22

"What if two identical cards appear, one in your hand and one in mine?" you want to know.

"That's all right. It took more than one deck to create the poster. We'll place a $10 bet on the outcome of each hand, and we'll continue to match our randomly picked hands until someone wins the whole hundred. Suppose your column is *B* and mine is *A*. We agree on some random method of selecting hands. If your hand turns out to be #8 and mine #1, I win — my straight beats your pair of fives. But if my hand is #4 and your hand is #9, you win — four sixes vs. a full house."

"What random method can we use to pick hands fairly from our columns?"

"I was just getting to that," I explain. "We could take numbers out of the phone book, one for you and one for me. Each would represent a position in our column, top to bottom, one through nine. Zero and we pick again. We could cut up this poster and glue the hands on large index cards, making three decks of nine cards each. Probably the best way is to use a standard deck, give you the ace, 2, 3, 4, 5, 6, 7, 8 and 9 of spades, and I'll take the same cards in hearts. Now we simply shuffle these two minidecks and turn over the top card from each stack. Ace represents the first (topmost) position, deuce the second, eight the eighth and so forth."

"That seems like a good solution," you agree. "Let's do it that way. But who gets the first choice of columns? Do we flip a coin? Since you already know which is the best column, it isn't fair for you to pick first.

"Quit complaining. I'll give you the first choice, but you only get ten minutes."

Okay, you've been a good sport so far, playing the imaginary game just the way I asked you to. Now that you've pretended yourself into this situation, take out your stopwatch and start timing. Study the illustration for ten minutes and then choose column *A, B,* or *C. Good luck.*

Welcome back. Which column did you choose?

If you picked A, I'll take *B.* Go ahead and shuffle our truncated decks (the spades and the hearts). Turn two cards over at a time, one from each stack, finding the corresponding hand on each column. The higher poker hand wins. Keep playing until all the cards have been exhausted, then reshuffle. When one of us gets $100 ahead, the bet is concluded.

Did you beat me? Possibly, but not likely. My column *B* was a definite favorite. It's simple to prove. For each two cards that we turn over, there are 81 possibilities. Any one of your nine cards could be paired against any one of my nine cards (9 × 9 = 81).

Look at these match-ups individually. The first hand in *A* beats five hands in column *B,* but loses to four others. The second *A* hand loses all nine confrontations. So far the score is 13-5, the advantage belonging to column *B.* Continue counting through the ninth hand in *A.* If you did this correctly, you tallied 39 victories for *A,* 42 for *B.* This means that *B* — my choice — has a 37ᶜ edge on every $10 bet. Whether or not you actually won the $100 wager *A* was the wrong side.

Maybe you picked *B.* In that case, my choice is *C.* Follow the procedure just explained, and you'll find that again you lose. Of the 81 possible match-ups between *B* and *C,* 42 belong to *C.*

This is where you get to look me in the eyes and swear that you honestly and truly chose column *C.* Did you actually analyze the previous two contests, proving that *B* was better than *A* and *C* better than *B?* Were you really able to do this within 10 minutes? If so, congratulations! You've demonstrated a remarkable degree of analytical ability under time-pressure conditions.

Is that the whole secret? In order to determine the strength of columns, would you itemize the outcomes of all possible matches?

No, that isn't the secret, and *C* isn't the answer!

What? Haven't we just proven that *C* is best? Didn't *A* get eliminated when pitted against *B?* Didn't *C* then beat *B* to become the obvious champion?

Well, go ahead and choose *C.* I'll take *A.* Who wins? You, maybe, if you got lucky; but you've just learned and you'll find that *A* is stronger by a 42-39 margin!

Surprised? Of course, but you're in good company. Even the world's most successful gamblers have accustomed themselves to thinking in terms of ascendance. Whether it's heads-up poker or football power ratings, they enjoy demoting the loser and elevating the winner, eventually arriving at a final victory — the king of the hill. The traditional elimination tournament is based on this concept. It works most of the time.

It didn't work in the example, though, did it? That's an exception to the ladder-of-power approach — an exception known to me and my poker students as Caro's Conception. Although I could have named it after myself, for the sake of modesty I've elected to honor my father.

So far you've learned an artistic hustle you ought to add to your gambling arsenal. I'm hoping that you'll understand the next level of application. Level Two is the realization that the Conception doesn't merely apply to carefully contrived puzzles. Contradictions to the traditional ladder-of-power notion exists all around you.

If Dallas is favored over Denver and Denver is favored over Baltimore, shouldn't Dallas be the choice over Baltimore? Probably, but not necessarily. It's possible for a football team or a poker player to possess weapons that are ideally suited to destroy certain opponents, but are ineffective against seemingly lesser foes. You normally won't be able to pinpoint the exact interaction of strengths and weaknesses that causes the unexpected outcome. When one team continually beats a substantially stronger team, to the surprise of the experts, there's a good chance that it's a fluke; but it might be an almost invisible interaction of factors. The prudent gambler should consider backing off from a bet if he's been wounded by a recurring but inexplicable event.

Suppose you're in a poker game with Felix the carpenter who never wins. Never beats anyone. Except *you,* and you're the best player at the table. Can't happen? Open your eyes! It *does* happen, and although it *may* be a fluke, you should give consideration to the possibility that your style of play is mixing with his in such a way that his few strengths have become inordinately powerful at the expense of your few weaknesses. Felix may accidentally and invisibly be getting the best of the situation. You should modify your style of play or stay out of his pots.

Caro's Conception at the Third Level is more difficult. You won't fully grasp it today, maybe not for a long time, maybe not ever. When you do, if you do, you'll begin to see the invisible. You'll view politics and personal relationships, baseball and boxing not in terms of ascending order, but as the total and complex blending of power and vulnerability — an arrangement of tangles and overlaps.

Here's a very simple example:

If you chose one card at random from each suit, then the clubs are 5-4 over the hearts and the diamonds are 5-4 over the clubs. And the lowly hearts? Why they're 5-4 over diamonds, of course!

When will you begin to understand Level Three? As soon as this ceases to amaze you.

Chapter 5

The Pain of Winning

"Poker is war!" my friend philosophized, pointing his finger so near to his girlfriend's mouth that she snapped at it playfully.

Undaunted by this disrespect, he paced to the farthest wall, pivoted and returned to where we were sitting, only to repeat, "Poker is war!"

"And war is hell," she teased, thinking he was acting too dramatic for the circumstance.

He seemed oblivious to her words. After all, he was about to invest $50 of his very own money to sponsor this woman in a small-limit poker game. Following several days of tutoring her in the finer points of poker, here was his final pep talk.

Incredibly, he said, "Poker is war!" for a third time.

Perhaps it's just as well that he did, because it is a very great truth. But then he told a terrible lie, a lie believed by millions of poker players.

This was the lie: "You're too sensitive for this game, Linda. You can't play good poker if you feel sorry for your opponents. Remember, those guys are trying to take your money, same as you're trying to take theirs. That's what the war's all about. So leave your feelings here, at home, and go win the money."

Linda left her feelings at home, but she lost the money.

It helps to be well versed on the mathematics and probability of poker. Even though a great deal of my published writing deals with the complicated statistical side of poker, I still think "tells" and psychology are vastly more important. That's why I never bother teaching poker to anyone who isn't keenly sensitive.

It's necessary to crawl into an opponent's mind — deep, deep inside — and decide whether he holds a strong hand or a weak hand. In order to do this, you must learn to *feel*. Feel his pain, agony, hope, desperation. When he offers you his very last dollar in a pot, you have to be willing to take it while, at the same time, knowing the hurt that pulses within him.

In my new book, *Book of Tells,* I show photographs depicting players in the act of "giving away" their hands. Thanks are due to the the two people who helped me most in assembling the book — Doyle Brunson, the former world poker champion, and Rick Greider, a superstar on the rise.

As a contributor to Doyle's 600-page poker bible, I wrote this about tells:

"Most people are prevented from living life as they want. In childhood, they're required to do chores they hate. They grow up having to conform at school. As adults they must shake hands they don't want to shake, socialize with people they dislike, pretend they're feeling 'fine' when they're feeling miserable and 'act' in control of situations where, in truth, they feel frightened and unsure.

"These people — the majority of folks you meet every day — are actors. They present themselves to you as people different than they really are.

"Deep within themselves they know they are not the same person they pretend to be. On an unconscious level, they think, 'Hey, I'm so phony that if I don't act to disguise my poker hand, people will see right through me!'

"And that's why the majority of these pitiful people are going to *give* you their money by always acting weak when they're strong and strong when they're weak."

To understand this, you have to feel some emotional pain. *In the world of poker psychology, it is not the callous who survive, it is the sensitive.*

Here's something that happened about a year ago. It isn't amusing or happy. It's not a funny anecdote or a clever diversion. A word of caution goes with it, a warning: This isn't for everyone. You may wish to send certain members of the family from the room until it's over.

I was between playing sessions, having coffee at Gardena's Rainbow Club. A man and a woman entered hand-in-hand and took the adjacent booth. He was a likable guy, but a terrible card player who gambled three or four times a week and seldom cashed out any chips.

Handsome, well-dressed and businesslike, he's one of those guys who seems compelled to lose. The woman? Mid-thirty and attractive, pretending to be very calm, but you knew better.

"Honey, why don't we go somewhere else for coffee? I know how much you like to play here and. . ."

"Don't worry, Julie. It's just a nice restaurant. That's the only reason I brought you here.

28

"Nothing is going to happen. I promise."

Perhaps this promise would have been kept had not Scott, a better-than-average poker player, happened along.

"Hi ya, Martin. There's a twenty lowball seat open. Great game, lotta loose money."

"Sorry, can't today. Me and my wife are driving up to Vancouver to see the sights for a couple of weeks."

I sipped my coffee and they theirs. Something monstrous was going to happen. You could sense it.

"Let me have a couple hundred worth of those traveler's checks."

"Martin, no!"

"Come on, Julie. Guy said the game's easy, you heard him. I'll just play for a few minutes. Maybe I can win a thousand. If I lose . . . well, two hundred won't hurt our plans much."

They debated this for a few minutes, and finally she weakened. Then she sat alone and waited. He came back after fifteen minutes bringing good news. "Winning six hundred. I told you it was going to be okay."

Promising to cash out within twenty minutes, he returned to the game. A half-hour passed before he reappeared. "I just got two big hands cracked," he sighed miserably, "I'm losing a little, about a hundred and a half. Better give me another two hundred."

Then he suggested that she go shopping and pick up some extra snacks for the trip. When she got back he'd be ready to leave, he said. He went back to his game, and a few minutes later I joined him, taking a seat across the table.

Are you following this? I mean, are you *really* following this? What we're discussing here is not just mild melodrama. We're talking about *pain,* the stuff of all tells.

Martin tried to play his best game. It didn't help, the cards were working against him. Once he held a highly respectable pat seven, and I drew to the perfect hand and connected. He nodded like a gentleman and pushed me the pot.

Inside, deep inside, he whimpered like a child and I felt it. His pain was so terrible it was almost tangible. When his pretty wife came to the table and saw that he had no more chips, she smiled. But you could tell the smile was cosmetic. She had a tell.

We're arriving at the point here, aren't we? Most tells, poker or otherwise, arise when someone is trying to cause you to reach a conclusion which differs from the truth.

Julie cashed more traveler's checks for her wounded husband, and then some more. His game was falling apart. When the last of his chips had vanished, he looked at me. "Would you ante for me one time for luck?" he pleaded.

This I did, of course, and then he lost and rose from the table. His wife had just approached to see how he was faring. She simply said, "Is it all gone? Everything?"

His silence was the affirmation. There would be no Vancouver this year. Before leaving the club, he bought her a candy bar. To me, this seemed like an inappropriate gesture. But they left holding hands.

In order to master the science of reading your opponents, you've got to feel what they feel. Sometimes, you've got to cope with the pain of winning.

Chapter 6

The Exaggeration Game

"The worst thing of all is I'm never lucky!"

Having so stated, Adam took a huge gulp of hot coffee. It seemed to me that he was deliberately trying to scald his innards. "Damn!" he shouted. "Damn, that's hot!" And he took another grimacing swallow, just to prove it.

"You wanna hear something really pathetic, M.J.C.?" he continued, using the initials that I'm known by around Gardena. Tears were bulging from his 29-year-old eyes. I guess it was because of the hot coffee, but who knows?

"Wanna hear something really pathetic?" he repeated.

Having just lost three important football bets, I could have handled *sad,* but not *pathetic.*

So I said, "I'll have to hear it some other time. I'm expecting someone any minute. Besides, I've got to make a phone call."

I began to rise diplomatically, but he clutched my sleeve and guided me back beside him.

"This'll just take a minute."

I waited. After about 15 seconds, he said, "Wanna hear it?"

"Sure."

"I'm in this 10 blind game. Everybody passes. Gets around to me. I'm dealing. I look at my hand. What do you think I've got?" He nudged me hard in the ribs.

"Ow! Easy. I don't know. What did you have?"

"Take a guess."

"A pat seven?"

"No! A six! A goddamn pat *six*! Six, five, one, two, three!" He tried another dramatic pause that didn't seem very effective.

I squirmed beside him, trying to determine my best strategy of escape.

"Did you hear what I said? A *six*! Pat!"

Obviously he wanted some sort of acknowledgement. "Wow! Those are hard to get. I suppose you got it beat." The odds are 286 to 1 against getting a 6-5-4-3-2 or better in Ace-to-Five Lowball (using Gardena's standard 53-card deck including the joker). So, indeed, Adam was talking about a semi-rare hand — one that you could expect to get only once in seven hours.

The reason I'd jumped ahead of his story and speculated that he'd lost with the hand is simple. In all my years of hearing lowball stories told by sad losers, I can't remember *even* hearing about a pat six that won!

"You're damn right I got it cracked! Listen to this, M.J.C. The blind calls. How many do you think he draws?"

"Three."

"That's right! Three friggin' cards! You hear about it from someone?"

"No, just guessing."

"Well, now guess what he made?"

"A wheel," I speculated. There were, of course, only two possible hands that could have beat Adam's 6-5-3-2-A, so I had a 50% chance to get this one right.

"No! A six-four!"

Damn! I thought. I'd started to say six-four.

Just at that instant my true friend Art Sathmary (known professionally as A.S.Q.) appeared.

Adam said, as I started to rise, "Just one more thing. Two hands later I get dealt —"

"Hi, A.S.Q.!" I greeted. I walked briskly away from Adam, muttering apologetically, "We're going to be late."

Maybe you feel this story is pointless. It contained no crisp climactic episode. It's just the sort of humdrum, slice-of-life thing that has no place in a sometimes serious gambling book. Is that what you're thinking?

Well the previous story was provided because it *is* mundane. Every experienced gambler hears this sort of thing all the time. The vocabulary of complaint, the language of misery, is universal. If you're a regular poker player, you can hear echos of similar tales right now.

Losers like to complain. Losing is a lonely experience. You suffer alone at a poker table. No one else seems aware of your tragedies. After the game, many humans need to share their agony.

In the Draw Poker section which I designed for Doyle Brunson's *A Course in Power Poker*, the final two pages are called "The Table of Sad

Stories."

Losers exaggerate. That's because they're not trying to convey *what really happened* so much as *how bad they feel*. You shouldn't challenge their outrageous claims of misfortune. Merely do your duty as a human being and commiserate.

A woman in A.S.Q.'s game once complained of having missed "17 flush draws in a row!"

"What are you talking about?" he corrected. "You just made one against me five minutes ago."

"Not in diamonds!" she raged.

Incidentally, the odds against missing 17 flushes consecutively aren't as great as most folks suppose. With the now-normal 53-card, joker-added deck, it's 52-1 against that happening. A standard 52-card deck (with which it's easier to miss) thins the odds to 36-1.

Anyhow, back to "The Table of Sad Stories," I collected the hard-luck claims of poker players and put them in a left-hand column headed "Miserable Misfortune." The right column consisted of the odds against it having *really* occurred. For instance, one of my favorite quotes from the table is: "Other folks have all the luck. This guy sits down, gets eleven straight pat hands and leaves."

The odds against that really happening are then given as: 1,686,574,119,000,000,000,000 to 1. That's figured for a deck that includes the joker. With a standard deck, this feat would be much, much tougher.

Even as it is, your chances of sitting down at a Gardena card table and legitimately getting a straight or better the first 11 hands in a row is. . . Well, let's say for the sake of simplicity — and because it's pretty close to the truth — that there are 4½ billion people on this planet.

That's a big number. It's 4500 times as large as a million. And a million's a pretty decent sum, don't you think? If I tell my computer to count, it whizzes through 1500 items each second. If I asked my computer to count to 4½ billion, it would take about 35 days. That's slow compared to very highspeed computers, but it's swift as far as you and I are concerned.

Well, enough of this. You can see that there are plenty of people in the world. Let's say every one of them sat down to play poker. The chances would be 374,794,250,000 to 1 against *even one* of them beginning with 11 straight pat hands (including four-of-a-kind). Even if the person having made this claim were the most honorable sort in the world, the chances of him having mentally malfunctioned far, far surpass the chances that this event actually took place.

Finally, after years and years of struggling to decipher what the world of poker complainers means by these bizarre assertions, I'm ready to announce my findings to the public. What follows is a sample of typical claims you're apt to hear from gamblers, and the truth.

Statement #1: "I can't believe it! I got 14 full houses beat in three hours!"

The truth: The speaker lost on one full house and on two flushes. Furthermore, he drew to two pair, sevens and fours, caught a seven and *would have lost* had he caught a four, since the opener had sixes-full. He's counting this as a loss, anyway, since he didn't hold three-of-a-kind in nearly an hour.

Statement #2: "I went to Vegas over the weekend. Must've played 21 for fifteen hours and never got a single blackjack!"

The truth: This person got about 40 blackjacks, perhaps less than his mathematical share. However, he only remembers 10 of them clearly, and these are hardly worth mentioning since he dumped $2000 playing keno.

Statement #3: "I would've hit the daily double. I had it figured cold, but I got tied up at the office."

The truth: The guy's second choice won the first half of the double. The horse that won the other race was a complete surprise. But now, looking back at the *Racing Form,* he can positively see why he might have picked it.

You see? It's human nature to feel you're running bad, even when you're not. Fluctuations for a gambler can be a lot greater than most informed people suppose. There's a lot of luck involved in games like gin rummy, poker and backgammon. That's why it's important to get as big an edge as possible.

There's one subject that no self-respecting gambling authority will discuss. It's the supernatural. Sure, it's easy to say that we have all the answers.

There are two main types of people who are screwing up my world: Those who claim to have discovered secret psychic answers; and those who blindly proclaim there can be no reality beyond that which they can fathom.

Both these groups, the fortune-tellers and the tunnel-vision scientists, are suffering from the same insanity. They both *need* answers. The former makes them up; the latter shouts that luck is understood by equation.

Nothing is more important to a gambler than whether unexplored phenomena might be influencing his luck.

Meanwhile, this is my advice. Get a good grasp of probabilities and gamble accordingly. Maybe there are undiscovered forces that guide our luck. But our best shot of winning the money right now is to deal with concepts we comprehend.

Here's a chart (below) to aid poker players. It is different from normal probability charts: Instead of giving you odds and percentages, which some find hard to understand, it tells you in hours and minutes how often you should expect certain hands. The assumption is that you're playing in a fairly brisk draw poker game with an average of 48 deals per hour. (The joker is included in the deck.)

Hand Dealt Pat	Expectancy, Once in
Five Aces	59,785 hours
Royal Flush	2,491 hours
Any Straight Flush	293 hours
Four-of-a-Kind	72 hours
Full House	13 hours, 41 minutes
Flush	7 hours, 40 minutes
Straight	2 hours, 55 minutes
Any complete hand *(including Four-of-a-Kind)*	1 hour, 46 minutes
Three-of-a-Kind	57 minutes
Two Pair	26 minutes
One Pair *(of Openers)*	8 minutes, 49 seconds
Jacks *(or better)*	5 minutes, 35 seconds

If you mistakenly expect to get a pat full house every hour, you're apt to feel miserable and cheated by fate. Your game will suffer. The table should help you maintain a realistic winning attitude.

Remember this: When you run bad, keep your luck secret. Getting sympathy from a fellow poker player is practically impossible.

This appropriate exchange of words happened two years ago in Reno. An elderly man slithered up to my friend and asked to borrow $20. "I lost my ass!" he explained.

My friend slapped him softly on the shoulders, whispered, "I hope you find it," and walked away.

PART THREE

Casino Games

"Holy Computer! There were seven
situations out of 120 where ties showed
a profit of 15% or more."

Chapter 7

The Great Baccarat Mystery

What have I done this time?

First, let me explain baccarat as briefly as I know how. There are two contenders, called *player* and *bank*. You may bet on either — or you can bet on a tie. The betting range is wide. For instance, at the Golden Nugget (Las Vegas) you can wager anywhere from $5 to $12,000 on either the player or the bank. Your bets on a tie can be from $5 to $1500. Both the Nugget and Binion's Horseshoe Club across the street recently added baccarat to their list of games.

Baccarat rules are easy. The player and the bank each get two cards. Every card has a point value ranging from 0 to 9. The 0-count cards are 10s and faces. Everything else is scored by spots: ace = 1, deuce = 2, nine = 9.

The strange thing about scoring baccarat scores is that only the last digit is considered. Therefore, 12 is the same as 2, and 17 is the same as 7. This means that if the player has two 9s and the bank has an ace and a 7, then the score is tied at 8.

There is absolutely no skill involved in the playing of a baccarat hand. Whether a side gets only the first two cards or receives a third card is determined by formula.

This is that formula:

(1) If either or both players have an 8-or 9-point total, then the game is over and a win or a tie is immediately paid; *otherwise,*

(2) The player always takes a third card *unless* he has 6 or 7 points.

(3) The bank always takes a third card with 0, 1 or 2 points;

(4) If the player stood on 6 or 7, then the bank always draws to 5 or less, otherwise, it stands.

(5) If the bank has 3, 4, 5 or 6 points *and* the player drew, then the value of the player's third card determines whether or not the bank draws:

Draws to 3: Always *unless* player's third card was an 8;
Draws to 4: If player's third card was 2, 3, 4, 5, 6 or 7;
Draws to 5: If player's third card was 4, 5, 6 or 7;
Draws to 6: If player's third card was 6 or 7.

Although these rules are simple once you're used to them, they're hard to visualize at first. Chart A shows how the bank draws in the event the player has taken a third card (see Figure 7).

Chart A
Does Bank Draw a Third Card?

Player's Third Card

	0	1	2	3	4	5	6	7	8	9
Bank Count = 3	Yes	Yes	Yes	Yes	Yes	Yes	Yes	Yes	No	Yes
Bank Count = 4	No	No	Yes	Yes	Yes	Yes	Yes	Yes	No	No
Bank Count = 5	No	No	No	No	Yes	Yes	Yes	Yes	No	No
Bank Count = 6	No	No	No	No	No	No	Yes	Yes	No	No

Figure 7

Remember (unless the game has already been decided because the player or the bank was dealt a "natural" 8 or 9 count), the bank *always* draws to 0, 1 or 2 points and *never* draws to 7.

Finally, you should know that if you bet $100 on the player, you can win $100 (the wager is even money), but if you bet $100 on the bank, you can only win $95. That's because the house takes a 5% commission on all bank bets. The reason for the commission is that, without it, all bank bets would show a profit. If you successfully bet a tie, you'll be paid 9 for 1 (8 to 1) on your money.

For a long time, most gamblers have grouped baccarat with games of pure chance such as craps and roulette. This is wrong. Baccarat is not a fixed-odds game where the house percentage doesn't vary from one bet to the next. Like blackjack, baccarat is affected by which cards remain in the shoe.

In March of 1982, David Sklansky projected that a winning counting system for baccarat might be devised. His stated objective was to point out the obvious, but not necessarily the practical. If the remaining shoe contained only 8s and 7s, then the bank would be heavily favored; if it contained only 3s and 2s, then the player would have a great edge.

If you mentally run through all possible outcomes with the combinations in Figure 7, you'll see why this is so.

Of course, there are even more extreme cases that prove that very rare remaining card combinations would be profitable. Suppose there were only face cards and 10s left in the deck. Not only would a tie be guaranteed, but you'd get 8 to 1 on your money!

A computer baccarat program that I've developed allows the user to select the cards remaining in the shoe, specify the number of hands to be dealt and then wait for the results. Separate versions of the same program do two other important tasks: (1) Determine how valuable each card denomination is in contributing toward a bank win, a player win, or a tie. (2) Randomly decide the last 20 cards remaining in the shoe and investigate to see if *any* bet is profitable at that point.

This last use of the program is extremely important. If a lot of winning situations can be isolated, then there's a good chance a practical count system can be devised. But if the winning situations are very rare, then a count system might not be worthwhile.

In 1983 I made this program available free to *Gambling Times* readers so that they could do their own pioneering research and then report back to me. As far as I know, that was the first time that any genuine gambling research program was made available to the public. The results should soon be known. Here, I'll show you some important stuff I've already discovered.

And even before that, I want to make this disclaimer. Note: This material was run by the Monte Carlo method, not by precise mathematical evaluation! The Monte Carlo method is a term used when the results are generated by random sample. A precise evaluation (such as the method I used to obtain all of my poker odds) yields an *exact* answer. Monte Carlo only yields an estimate—and the larger the sample, the closer to the truth it tends to be.

This baccarat program was developed on an Apple II computer using the Pascal programming language. It is, indeed, capable of running on higher-speed computers, but right now I've only used it on the Apple. This means I was limited in the number of hands I could generate. (The Apple program deals and analyzes 10,000 hands in 15 minutes.) The total scope of the hands generated for this report was one million.

In order to publish results with less fluctuation and with a higher degree of confidence, I will need to run a lot more trials, perhaps a billion! Nevertheless, the results are revealing and, almost certainly, they are close to what they should be.

Finally, I want to say that baccarat odds *can* be determined mathematically. There is really no need to deal hands at random. The formula for deciding how often each side will win for a given situation is not terribly difficult, but when you deal with thousands of situations, it's very time consuming. The formula itself can be programmed, and maybe I'll do that sometime in the future. By the way, I'd like to acknowledge some highly literate letters dealing with this subject, especially those from Mason Malmuth and Jack Howard.

Anyway, let's look at what we have so far.

True, if you can isolate a deck with *all* 3s and 2s or *all* 8s and 7s, then a winning bet can be made. But what if the deck is just heavy in these categories? Take a look at Figure 7-1.

```
Cards in shoe (by rank and quantity):
  K=32 Q=32 J=32 T=32 9=32 8=0 7=0 6=32 5=32 4=32 3=32
  2=32 A=32
AFTER 30,000 HANDS...
*****************************************
*   SIDE      DECISIONS     RETURN    *
*-------------------------------------*
*  Player     13,438        -0.47%    *
*   Bank      13,580        -1.79%    *
*   Ties       2,982       -10.54%    *
*****************************************
```

Figure 7-1

Here I've simply started with the full eight-deck shoe and eliminated all the 8s and 7s. Since 8s and 7s favor the bank, this should help the player. It does. But, alas, not enough to win — the player's return on investment is still −0.4%, which is a loss of 47 cents for every $100 wagered.

Incidentally, the traditionally accepted percentages on baccarat are -1.16% betting the bank and -1.37% betting the player. My figures will average slightly better results than these for both sides. That's because mine consider a tie to be a 0% return on investment, while traditional calculations treat a tie as nonexistent. My method is correct.

Now let's leave the 3s and 2s out of the shoe. (See Figure 7-2.) This should help the bank — and it does. But after 30,000 deals, we see that a bet on the bank lost .46 percent for every $100 wagered.

```
Cards in shoe (by rank and quantity):
 K=32 Q=32 J=32 T=32 9=32 8=32 7=32 6=32 5=32 4=32 3=0
2=0 A=32
AFTER 30,000 HANDS...
**********************************
*   SIDE      DECISIONS     RETURN  *
*---------------------------------*
*  Player      13,261      -1.85%  *
*   Bank       13,815      -0.46%  *
*   Ties        2,924     -12.28%  *
**********************************
```

Figure 7-2

Oh, well, let's try some more exotic combinations, such as those which might occur toward the bottom of the shoe. (Casinos deal out almost the entire shoe — until there are about 16 cards remaining in the deck. Additionally, from 1 to 10 cards are often burned to begin a new shoe — randomly determined by the denomination of the top card— so these are never known to a baccarat counter.)

Suppose you got down to the last of the shoe and all the cards were evenly distributed except the 8s, 7s, 3s and 2s. There were four each remaining of all other denominations. However, there were six each of the 3s and 2s and only two each of the 8s and 7s. Shouldn't this win for the player? (See Figure 7-3.) Too bad. As you can see, this situation offers no winning bet.

```
Cards in shoe (by rank and quantity):
  K=4 Q=4 J=4T=4 9=4 8=2 7=2 6=4 5=4 4=4 3=6 2=6 A=4

AFTER 5,000 HANDS...
***********************************
*   SIDE      DECISIONS     RETURN  *
*----------------------------------*
*  Player       2,232       -1.10%  *
*   Bank        2,287       -1.19%  *
*   Ties          481      -13.42%  *
***********************************
```

Figure 7-3

After running 50 of these mini-trials, I found no winning situations
which you could reasonably expect to happen frequently. But that didn't
mean there were none, so the investigation continued.

Next, I went to sleep and let the computer keep working. Its task was
to deal down to the last 20 cards, print out what those cards were, deal
2500 hands, print the result and tell me whether there was a possible
profit. That number of hands is not sufficient, of course, but it allowed the
computer to investigate a large number of random situations and call the
winners to my attention. Then I could investigate further.

Although this next part will surprise some readers, statisticians will
merely yawn. Out of 120 situations investigated, 76 showed a profit for
the player, the bank or a tie. But, you see, most of these were flukes, with
profits of less than 2%. A sample of 2500 hands is small enough that
you'd get a big percentage of winners even dealing from a normal shoe.
It takes a while for things to even out.

Naturally, I only investigated the situations with the highest winning
percentage. Excluding ties, the biggest profit was 4% for the player.
(See Figure 7-4.) But a look at the card distribution showed no rational
reason why this run should have favored the player so heavily. Indeed,
when I followed this up with a larger run of 30,000 hands, the profit
vanished. (See Figure 7-5.)

```
          Computer selects last 20 cards remaining in shoe
Cards in shoe (by rank and quantity):
  K=1 Q=2 J=0 T=1 9=1 8=0 7=2 6=1 5=3 4=3 3=2 2=2 A=2
    POSSIBLE PROFIT! WINNING SITUATIONS = 54 OUT OF 81
AFTER 2,500 HANDS...
*********************************************
*   SIDE        DECISIONS       RETURN    *
*-----------------------------------------*
*  Player        1,163          4.00%     *
*   Bank         1,063         -6.13%     *
*   Ties           274         -1.36%     *
*********************************************
```

Figure 7-4

```
Cards in shoe (by rank and quantity):
  K=1 Q=2 J=0 T=1 9=1 8=0 7=2 6=1 5=3 4=3 3=2 2=2 A=2
AFTER 30,000 HANDS...

*********************************************
*   SIDE        DECISIONS       RETURN    *
*-----------------------------------------*
*  Player       13,203         -0.71%     *
*   Bank        13,416         -1.53%     *
*   Ties         3,381          1.43%     *
*********************************************
```

Figure 7-5

Other good leads similarly disappeared. My hunch is that *real* winning opportunities are very scarce and, even when they appear, the percentage edge is usually very small.

Even if you had a high-speed computer at the baccarat table, you might not stumble on enough profitable situations to make a very good living. Any count system could only approximate the work of the computer and would never be as accurate.

What's the bottom line on betting either the bank or the player? Development of a worthwhile winning system is not impossible, but it's unlikely.

But don't lose hope, there's better news coming.

My final experiment took an entirely different approach. I began to wonder: If you dealt a lot of hands, what cards would contribute most to a player win, a bank win or tie? Figure 7-6 is the result of my first run of 30,000. The numbers show how many times each denomination of card contributed toward a result. For instance, in all the hands that the bank won, there were 5302 deuces involved. Overall, the bank did better than expected for this run, losing only about half a percent.

This shows again that 30,000 is not enough hands to be sure of the conclusions. Another way to tell that 30,000 is insufficient is to see the differences among the kings, queens, jacks, and 10s. Obviously these should be about equal in the long run.

After running five separate trials, totaling 150,000 hands, here are some conclusions. The 7s and 6s were about 2% less common than other cards when the player won. (I had expected to see 8s and 7s the rarest.) No card contributed greatly to a player win. No trend could be discovered for the bank, although 8s and 7s did appear slightly more often when the bank won.

Something exciting happened with ties. During the 150,000 hands, 7s and 6s contributed to ties 11% more often than other denominations! This was unexpected. You might think that face cards and 10s would be the main contributors, but they appeared less than their share of the time!

Armed with this unexpected discovery, I searched the earlier random runs to see if the computer had uncovered any shoes where ties prospered.

```
      Randomly deals and charts how card-ranks affect outcome
    Cards in shoe (by rank and quantity): NORMAL 8-DECK SHOE
    CARD
    CONTRIBUTING TO      PLAYER WIN      BANK WIN      TIE
    ---------------------------------------------------------
        King ............. 5066            5303         1001
      Queen ............. 5098            5227         1056
       Jack ............. 5162            5208         1026
        Ten ............. 5142            5226         1004
       Nine ............. 5175            5174         1028
      Eight ............. 5081            5280         1049
      Seven ............. 4979            5188         1230
        Six ............. 4941            5238         1196
       Five ............. 5057            5229         1106
       Four ............. 5128            5207         1065
      Three ............. 5059            5234         1108
      Deuce ............. 5101            5302          991
        Ace ............. 5114            5233         1034

    AFTER 30,000 HANDS...

    ******************************************
    *   SIDE        DECISIONS      RETURN    *
    *----------------------------------------*
    *  Player       13,328         -1.79%    *
    *    Bank       13,866         -0.52%    *
    *    Ties        2,806        -15.82%    *
    ******************************************
```

Figure 7-6

Holy computer! There were seven situations out of 120 where ties showed a profit of 15% or more. Five of these were rich in 7s and 6s, but two were not, so I ran 5000 hands of an oddball first, to see if it was only a fluke. It was, showing a large loss this time.

One run showed a huge 59.84% profit, and the distribution looked extremely favorable — almost all face cards, 8s and 6s. There was one really peculiar profit which was primarily rich in small cards. (See Figure 7-7.) A longer run of 5000 showed almost the same result (28.88% profit). Maybe there are common combinations without 6s, 7s or 0-counts that favor ties.

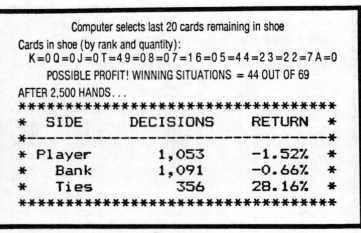

```
            Computer selects last 20 cards remaining in shoe
Cards in shoe (by rank and quantity):
  K=0 Q=0 J=0 T=4 9=0 8=0 7=1 6=0 5=4 4=2 3=2 2=7 A=0
    POSSIBLE PROFIT! WINNING SITUATIONS = 44 OUT OF 69
AFTER 2,500 HANDS...
************************************
*  SIDE        DECISIONS       RETURN   *
*---------------------------------------*
*  Player      1,053         -1.52%  *
*   Bank       1,091         -0.66%  *
*   Ties         356         28.16%  *
************************************
```

Figure 7-7

Here are my very preliminary conclusions (most will probably be correct; some may eventually be proven wrong):

(1) A counting system to bet on the bank or the player is impractical (although rare winning situations occur).

(2) A counting system designed to find favorable tie situations can almost certainly be developed.

(3) The ranks 7 and 6 contribute heavily to ties.

(4) The shoe contains favorable tie situations often enough to make large profits if all the information were available to the gambler.

(5) It is not specific cards, so much as it is *combinations* of cards, that warp the odds for certain bets. This makes counting difficult, because the value of each card remaining depends on all the other cards remaining. Therefore, a shoe heavy in low cards can be beneficial to ties, even if no 7s or 6s are present.

(6) Probably (but not for certain), if you count face cards and 10s as neutral, then a deck heavy in high cards *or* a deck heavy in low cards favors a tie.

(7) As a general rule, if the remaining deck contains 75% face cards, 10s, 7s and 6s, then I would consider betting a tie.

(8) If the deck contains 67% (two-thirds) 5s, 4s, 3s, 2s, and As, I would consider betting a tie.

(9) If the deck contains 50% 6s and 7s, I would consider betting a tie — but this is dangerous with many combinations.

(10) The previous advice is very, very preliminary. There are probably much better ways to measure. For instance, a count of 7s down through As might have advantages, ignoring face cards and 10s.

Baccarat investigation is not on my schedule. In fact, if I were to spend a lot of time on it, I would pursue a mathematical rather than a Monte Carlo method. These results came about because I was developing a video game called Baccarat Adventure, and the tools to do this research were already available.

I think it would be great fun if readers continued this project. Baccarat isn't as involved as poker, so if some of you feel the urge to do the calculations, there may be a profit in it.

I'm making my computer baccarat programs available to any reader up until July 1, 1985.

These programs run only on Apple computers with the language system. You must have Pascal, because I provide only the programs, not the computer language. There is a $5 charge to cover the cost of the floppy disk and shipping. However, if you send your own blank disk and include the return postage and packaging, it's absolutely free.

You must agree to send me the *results!* All investigation you do becomes my property to publish or use without charge as I please. (I will, of course, give credit where I feel it is warranted.)

As far as I know, this is the first time any genuine gambling research program has been made available to the public.

I'd also like to receive calculations and ideas from those without computers. My mail indicates that my readers are among the most sophisticated on the planet. Prove it!

So long!

Chapter 8

Video Poker

Andrew sat down to play video poker on my home computer. He punched in a $5 bet and the first hand he got was...

"This isn't going to be my day," said he. Telling my computer to throw away everything, he waited four-tenths of a second until the screen gobbled up the cards and replaced them with Eight-Four of Clubs, Five of Spades and Six-Seven of Diamonds. The computer chimed merrily for several seconds and announced a Straight. It paid him $20 (a $15 profit) and prompted him to wager again.

"All right!" he gloated.

But "All right" was not an appropriate remark, because all was not *right*. Oh, sure, the computer program was functioning perfectly and the weather was mild and I'd had a good day at poker. Still, a tingle rode up my spine as I realized that a lot of people would have drawn exactly the way Andrew had — five cards.

And, yet, this was terribly, hopelessly, tragically wrong! Imagine the chagrin, the utter shock to the spirit, had Andrew realized that manner of blunder he had committed! Here was a fairly skilled poker player and you'd think he'd know enough to draw four. But again, maybe it was understandable, because poker players never need face that decision in normal poker.

You see, video poker is a lot different than the customary kind of poker. You don't raise, bluff or use psychology. And you play *every* hand! If this sounds like there's no skill to it, guess again. These machines are all over the casinos.

I watched Andy challenge the machine I had turned my computer into. It was a fully functioning video poker machine that played and paid exactly like the progressive jackpot poker machines in Vegas.

It had been devised for the sole purpose of writing on this subject. Its primary function was to analyze various draws, finding whether it is better, say, to draw two to a pair of queens or throw away a queen and draw one to a Straight Flush. Most of these things can be done better with just a calculator and an understanding of probability, but there are some strategies that I wanted to let the computer try out while I slept.

Somewhere along the road, I'd gotten sidetracked, and the program was being used mostly as a game with the color graphics I'd added. My machine does lots more than the video machines in Las Vegas. It investigates, keeps track of your winnings, analyzes your results, allows you to select the speed of the deal and even provides an instant replay of the last hand on request.

But with folks coming over to try it out, I kept thinking my scientific program had somehow been demoted in status to an entertainment device.

Oh well, so be it. . . Andrew had just drawn three cards to a Queen-Jack of Hearts. He caught garbage. "Poor Andy!" said the computer.

This wasn't all wasted time for me. I watched four people play my machine this past week. What astounds me is that the same mistakes kept occurring over and over.

I guess I'd better tell you how to play right. After all, we're friends, aren't we? This is going to be a preliminary report. It deals specifically with one machine — a *progressive jackpot machine* of a standard type found in Las Vegas.

Here's how it works.

You put in from one to five coins, usually quarters. The computer deals a five-card poker hand on a video screen. By pressing buttons you now instruct the computer to either hold a card or throw it away. You can keep all your cards or throw away as many as you want. The machine then replaces the cards you hate, frequently with some you hate even more.

"Progressive" means that the jackpot keeps growing as more bets are made. Sometimes jackpots get very large — over $10,000. So, what must you do to win? A Royal Flush will do the trick. That's not quite as difficult as it seems, because you play every hand and you can draw to a Straight Flush instead of some other combination whenever you think it's wise.

Right now, I'm going to give some straight advice, dazzle you with some figures and set you loose on the casinos with a favorable expectation.

Good thing you've got me for a friend.

Speaking of friends, David Sklansky wrote a tentative report on video poker not many months ago. It appeared in Volume #15 of *Casino and Sports*. As always, David's insights and the quality of his research were monumental. In this chapter I will take you even beyond David's pioneering work.

There are many varieties of poker machines, paying different amounts. The one under discussion is among the most liberal and most popular. Here's what it pays:

	(Jackpot for five coins)
Royal Flush	250 for 1
Straight Flush	50 for 1
Four-of-a-Kind	25 for 1
Full House	8 for 1
Flush	5 for 1
Straight	4 for 1
Three-of-a-Kind	3 for 1
Two Pair	2 for 1
Jacks, Queens	
Kings, Aces	1 for 1
	(You get your bet back)

Try to find a machine that gives these payoffs. Remember, you're not eligible for the jackpot unless you bet the maximum — five coins. This means $1.25 on the most popular quarter machines.

So . . .

Video Poker Rule #1: *Always bet five coins.*
You will improve your chances dramatically by drawing correctly to your hands. Seemingly innocuous mistakes can, in fact, be very costly in the long run. And, keep in mind, a one-cent or two-cent error in strategy will amount to a lot in a hurry. If you're used to playing home poker at a pace of 30 hands an hour, forget it. You can play so fast your fingers will whimper!

As you probably realize, there's another element to winning besides drawing correctly, and that's finding a machine with a big enough jackpot.

David tells me that $3000 is about the break-even point for a quarter machine. That means a jackpot of 2400 for 1, $12,000 on a dollar machine.

Video Poker Rule #2: *Find the biggest jackpot you can.*
It's a mistake to look for a lucky machine. If you see one slapping down lots of full houses, that doesn't mean it's in a "cycle." The machines are not programmed for cycles, they are programmed to give a fair shuffle, which, by the way, is a lot more thorough than any human shuffle. Or, at least, it is on my computer.

The first thing you should know... Let me take that back. You don't really need to know this at all, but it's interesting. The first question of interest is: *How much would an ape lose playing this machine? Or, How much would you lose if you were playing blindfolded?*

Turns out I have an answer to that question. If the jackpot is the recommended minimum size ($3000), then you will lose two-thirds of your money (getting 33.592 cents back for every dollar you bet). That figure is pretty stable even for a small jackpot (it begins at $1000 every time the previous one is claimed).

The computer game is only risking the $1000 it originally put into the jackpot. All additions to the jackpot come out of the players' wagers. If you decided in advance that you were going to stand pat on every hand, your mathematical return would be $1 for every $3 bet.

All right, that's the *worst* we can do. Let's improve on it.

Video Poker Rule #3: *Never keep a kicker.*
Let's say you've put your money in a machine and got dealt this hand...

Veteran poker players invariably consider drawing two, discarding the eight and six.

Whenever poker is played correctly anywhere in the Milky Way, you've got to have a *reason* to keep a kicker. What would be your reason here? Could make Aces-up, you say? True, but Aces-up is no better than Kings-up. In video poker, two pair is two pair, and sixes and fours are just the same as aces and queens. While watching my friends play my machine, I was surprised at how many kickers were kept.

Reason it out. If you draw three to kings, what's the worst thing that could happen on the first card you catch? It could be a deuce, right? Wrong! The worst thing would be if it were of the rank you threw away. That would mean your hopes of pairing that card would be only two-thirds as good as if you'd caught a card such as a ten. So, you *could* be slightly worse off by not keeping the ace kicker. But the difference is negligible.

The thing that's terrific about *not* keeping the kicker is that you have a nearly 50% better chance of catching a third king. And that pays 3 to 1. Remember, *Rule #1* applies to three-of-a-kind, also.

As my friends tried out my machine, they wrote down hands that gave them problems. One that was listed by three out of the four players was this. . . Is it better to draw three cards to a Royal, keeping a Ten, or Four to a face card?

Here's an illustration . . .

By the way, don't even consider drawing two to the small straight. Your choice is four to the Jack of Hearts or three to the Jack-Ten of Hearts.

What would you do? The thing to keep in mind is that far more money is paid out by the machine for one pair of Jacks, Queens, Kings or Aces than for any other kind of hand. So by throwing the Ten away, you get an extra shot at making a pair of Jacks. On the other hand you sacrifice your shot at the jackpot, because you can no longer make a Royal Flush.

Hey, Mike, could you tell me approximately how hard it is to make that three-card Royal? Sure, I'll do better than that... I'll tell you *exactly* how hard it is. It's 16,214 to 1 against it. So it seems that this chance might be too remote to merit keeping the Ten. But is it? There's only one way to know for sure. It's to find out just how much you'll get back for a dollar's worth of bet if you draw three. And how much if you draw four.

This is the breakdown:

If you draw four to the Jack of Diamonds...

(178,365 possible combinations of cards)

Hand Made	Winning Combinations	Penny Value
Royal Flush	0	0.00
Straight Flush	0	0.00
Four-of-a-Kind	52	0.73
Full House	216	0.97
Flush	330	0.93
Straight	832	1.87
Three-of-a-Kind	4,102	6.90
Two Pair	8,874	9.95
Pair Jacks...Aces	45,456	25.49
Value: 46.8 cents.		

Now, what if you draw only three cards, keeping the Jack-Ten of Diamonds?

(16,215 possible combinations of cards)

Hand Made	Winning Combinations	Penny Value
Royal Flush	1	14.80
Straight Flush	3	0.93
Four-of-a-Kind	2	0.31
Full House	18	0.89
Flush	161	4.97
Straight	252	6.22
Three-of-a-Kind	281	5.20
Two Pair	711	8.77
Pair Jacks...Aces	2,955	18.22
Value: 60.3 cents.		

Just like that we've learned it's much better to keep the Ten and draw three to the Royal. This shows you a means of itemizing all possible results and determining the correct strategy. You see, it isn't guesswork; it's science. The manner in which these combinations of hands were derived is beyond the scope of this book. However, the same precise method was used in formulating this overall strategy.

In this previous example, it's important to point out that this particular four-card draw was handicapped *because* the suited Ten was discarded. Normally a four-card draw to a Jack returns about 48%, depending on the ranks and suits of the discards.

So...

Video Poker Rule #4: *Never draw four if you can draw three to a Royal.*

If you have a hand like...

you could think about drawing four to the Queen. Certainly that's better than drawing four to the damaged Jack. But, still, it's better to draw to the Royal, even if the jackpot is only $1000 (in which case you shouldn't be playing). You might consider drawing two, but that's also wrong.

Now look at this...

Forget about drawing two to the Flush. That's a real loser. The question is, should you draw two cards or three cards in this case? If you drew two, which cards would you keep? The answer is keep the Queen and Jack because the Straight opportunities for King and Queen are fewer (because it's more dead-ended on the high side).

(By the way, for the above reason, a four-card draw to a Jack is slightly better than a four-card draw to a Queen. And Kings and Aces are still worse—though equally so.)

It happens that the answer to the previous problem is to draw only two. That returns 51% as compared to 49% for a three-card draw.

Video Poker Rule #5: *Don't break a flush to draw one to a straight flush.*

This is a common mistake.

Here's your hand...

The pat hand is already worth a 500% return. That is, your original $1.25 and an additional $5.00. So right now you're getting back $6.25. How much comes back if you draw?

You'd get $2.66 worth of Straight Flush, 80 cents worth of ordinary Flush and 8 cents worth of Jacks. We're talking about $3.54 here; and we're paying $6.25 to draw. You see, that one isn't even close!

And for the same reason, though not quite as compelling...

Video Poker Rule #6: *Never break a straight to draw to a straight flush.*

Of course, a video poker machine does not consider a Royal Flush to be the same thing as a Straight Flush. If it's a Royal we're talking about, then that's completely different. In fact...

Video Poker Rule #7: *Always break a flush to draw to a royal.*

Video Poker Rule #8: *Always break a straight to draw to a royal.*

These last two rules imply something so obvious I won't bother to make a rule out of it: Always break a pair to draw to a Royal.

But this isn't so obvious...

Video Poker Rule #9: *Always break anything to draw to a royal.* (This assumes the jackpot is David's minimum $3000 or higher for a quarter machine.)

It is my opinion that you can beat a machine with a jackpot even smaller than $3000, but I'm not sure yet.

It's important to realize that there is a theoretical time when the jackpot gets so big that you would break any hand and draw like crazy. For instance, if the jackpot were $20,000,000, that's big enough to throw away a pat 9-high Straight Flush and draw five. No, $19,000,000 is *not* big enough! Use this strategy which works even better as the jackpot increases beyond $3000.

Video Poker Rule #10: *Never draw five if you have any card larger than a ten.*

Remember Andrew at the beginning of this book? He violated this rule and look where it got him. (He made a Straight!) Well, it's right in the long run, I promise.

Video Poker Rule #11: *Don't keep a ten for a four-card draw.*

These rules and the related advice given are not intended to cover all aspects of video poker. A discussion of each dilemma you're apt to face would require a book-length volume. Some research is still not complete.

Let's say the jackpot is $3000 for your $1.25 bet. What is it worth to you to be drawing one to a Royal Flush? It turns out there are three different Royals you can draw to ranging in return-per-dollar from $52.36 to $53.57. The best one you can hope for is King-Queen-Jack-Ten. The average of these three types is $52.79 per dollar, and on your $1.25 bet means the value of your situation before you draw is $65.99. Therefore, if someone sneaks up behind you and offers $50 to take over your hand, you should not sell it.

It occurs to me money could be made by approaching players and offering to buy hands before the draw. In that light, here are some interesting stats.

With five quarters already invested:

A one-card draw to an open-end Straight Flush is worth $4.23, plus 8 cents for every card higher than a Ten.

A one-card draw to an inside Straight Flush is worth $2.71, plus 8 cents for every card higher than a Ten.

A one-card draw to a full house is worth $3.14.

A one-card draw to a flush is worth $1.20, plus 8 cents for every card higher than a Ten.

A one-card draw to an open-end straight is worth 85 cents plus 8 cents for every card higher than a Ten.

A one-card draw to an inside-straight is worth 43 cents (rounded off — it's actually worth exactly half an open-end straight) plus 8 cents for every card higher than a Ten.

This last item is fairly interesting. It means that if you hold...

you will get 75 cents back out of your $1.25 on average if you draw one. Earlier in this report you learned that a two-card draw to three high cards was better than either a three-card or a four-card draw. The two-card draw, remember, returns 51%. On a $1.25 wager, that comes to only 64 cents. It's clearly better to draw one.

However, if two of these four high cards are suited (and they will be 91% of the time), you should draw three to the Royal. (That is, unless the jackpot is not much above our recommended minimum of $3000.)

Here's what your hand is worth for a $1.25 bet on some other draws: A two-card draw to Three-of-a-Kind is worth $5.57; three to a pair of Jacks, $2.30; three to a pair of sixes, $1.41.

A two-card draw to King-Queen-Jack is worth 64 cents. Note that drawing to Ace-King-Queen is not as good due to diminished Straight possibilities. (In fact, it's only worth 56 cents.) Still, it's better to draw two than three, unless two of these cards are suited.

A two-card draw to a Flush is only worth 38 cents whereas a five-card draw is worth about 45 cents. I'm not sure of the precision of this last figure. It depends on which cards you throw away. Once you've thrown away five garbage cards, your chances of snatching something worthwhile are better than from a full deck of 52 cards. Don't forget, right now the return we're dealing with is per $1.25. A *return-per-dollar* on a five-card draw is only about 36 cents.

If you'd rather deal in dollars altogether, convert the figures on this list by dividing by 5 and then multiplying by 4.

For your $1.25, a two-card Straight draw like 9-8-7, discarding 4-2, is worth 34 cents. Obviously, you should draw five instead. Three cards to Queen-Jack returns 64 cents; to King-Queen or King-Jack, 62 cents; to Ace-King, Ace-Queen or Ace-Jack, 60 cents.

A four-card draw to a Jack returns 60 cents (and varies slightly depending on your discards; throwing a suited Ten brings it down 1.8 cents). Four to an Ace or King is worth 59 cents and four to a Queen is in between.

Now let's take this information and make it win.

Following, you'll find my *Baby Steps for Best Profit*. Take it to the casino if you want. As you get familiar with the routine, the procedure will become automatic. Do exactly as instructed.

Video Poker

Mike Caro's
"BABY STEPS FOR BEST PROFIT"

(Quarter machine with $3000 jackpot)

If you don't want to play a hand then quit
Otherwise continue
Insert five coins and play

"GLORY GROVE"

If you have a Royal Flush then stand pat and start over
Otherwise continue
If you have four cards of a Royal Flush then draw one and start over
(Even if this means breaking up a King-high Straight Flush)
Otherwise continue
If you have a Straight Flush then stand pat and start over
Otherwise continue
If you have a Straight then stand pat and start over
Otherwise continue
If you have at least four of the same suit then skip to "Garden of One Color"
Otherwise continue
If you have any paired cards then skip to "Land of Companions"
Otherwise continue

"LONGSHOT LOBBY"

If you have three cards of a Royal Flush then draw two and start over
Otherwise continue
If you have an open-end Straight opportunity then draw one and start over
Otherwise continue
If you have two cards of a Royal Flush then draw three and start over
Otherwise continue

If you have King-Queen-Jack then draw two and start over
Otherwise continue
If you have two cards higher than a Ten then draw three and start
over
Otherwise continue
If you have a card higher than a Ten then draw four and start over
Otherwise continue
If you have three cards of a Straight Flush then draw two and start
over
Otherwise continue
Draw five and start over

"GARDEN OF ONE COLOR"

If you have a Flush then stand pat and start over
Otherwise continue
If you have three cards of a Royal Flush then draw two and start over
Otherwise continue
If you have four cards of a Straight Flush then draw one and start
over
Otherwise continue
If you have a pair higher than Tens then draw three and start over
Otherwise continue
Draw one to your Flush and start over

"LAND OF COMPANIONS"

If you have Four-of-a-Kind or a Full House then stand pat and start
over
Otherwise continue
If you have Three-of-a-Kind then draw two and start over
Otherwise continue
If you have three cards of a Royal Flush then draw two and start over
Otherwise continue
If you have two pair then draw one and start over
Otherwise continue
Draw three to your pair and start over

You can try this strategy on quarter-machine jackpots ranging from $2500 to $5000, but you'll have to shop around. Some categories of hands have been lumped together even though the return varies. Example: Drawing to 9-8-7 suited returns about 60%, but 9-8-5 returns just about 40%. Due to their rarity, I call them both two-card draws to Straight Flushes. Nevertheless, if you follow these "Baby Steps" exactly, you will NEVER make a significant mistake. Finally, when the "Steps" say to draw you will sometimes need to make obvious choices. For instance, if you have two 3-card Royal draws, K-Q and J-10, you would keep the K-Q.

Chapter 9

Future Keno?

"If you know so much about keno, how come you can't beat it?" Elaine shot this question at me with a smug defiance as she x'd the numbers 56, 79 and 80 on her card.

It occurred to me that I'd been undiplomatic in attacking her favorite game. Still, this sometimes-bright college woman *had* asked me to teach her about gambling while she was in Vegas, so what did she expect.

"Elaine," I said in my softest voice, "nobody beats keno."

I waited for these words to register. The wait was short.

"My uncle beats it," she argued.

You do not persist in the face of this sort of irrationality. The correct strategy is to back off and wait for a time when the person will respond to reason. Whenever someone makes statements such as Elaine's that person does not want to be persuaded. That person wants to be cradled by whatever faith or whatever magic seems comforting. If you try to destroy that faith or that magic without permission you will meet a hostile, unyielding enemy. This, my friends, is a great truth.

So, observing this great truth, I held silent and watched Elaine at play. There would come a better time for mathematical truth and scientific explanation.

"I can't believe it!" she moaned. "Three numbers and I didn't hit a single one of them out of twenty!"

"You're really running bad," I soothed. "Let's try something else."

She smiled now, confident again that I was on her side. So she nodded her assent and we were off to try something more rational, something called blackjack. On the way, of course, Elaine dropped a few quarters into a slot machine which stood pandering too near to the aisle. Six quarters were digested.

Blackjack was hardly better than break-even, but at least (by averaging her win with my loss) we made a few dollars. Such is the soul of gambling.

Anyway, I didn't get to tell Elaine the harsh truth about keno. She wouldn't have listened, but you will.

Keno, keno . . . What can you say about keno? You can say: Numbers fascinate even the non-mathematical. You can say: Eighty squares can be divided into eight rows, each 10 squares across. You can ask: Who are those guys who sit around watching the numbers light up when they could be out in the woods feeding the antelope?

I'll tell you what's so great about keno. You don't have to wait half an hour between races. You don't have to concentrate on keeping track of the cards as they whizz by while you wonder whether to increase your blackjack bet. You don't need to look deep into the spirit of a poker opponent and guess whether or not he's bluffing.

You can just sit around in a comfortable chair and drink yourself stupid, secure in the knowledge that you're still as talented as any other keno player in the whole damn world. You can lose your 20% to 30% with the best of them, and because you're only betting a buck or two a game, it's not even as expensive as it is for those sophisticated craps shooters who boast of only having a one-percent disadvantage. You can watch them spend themselves broke chasing that bargain.

That having been said, keno still bores me. Though it has devoted followers, I think it would have even more groupies if it packed more number-by-number excitement.

Here's the problem as I see it. The numbers go from one to 80. When you watch a keno board, one number comes up at a time. Say you've picked six numbers. The chances are 74-6 against any of your numbers being lit after the first ball is chosen. That means almost all players suffer an initial disappointment.

Successful games with mass appeal generally work the opposite. In fact, I've devised a keno prototype for my computer where, in addition to the regular tickets, players can bet in two other ways.

The first is a *score* game where the odd numbers play the even numbers. Beside the keno board is a separate scoreboard. One half is marked *odd* and the other *even*. Above this scoreboard is a slot where the last number picked is displayed. If that number is even, it is added to the right column; if it is odd it is added to the left column.

On my game you can make an even-money bet for any amount up to

66

$500 (pretend money, of course), but the player must bet on *odd*. So where is the house edge? Aren't there 40 even numbers and 40 odd numbers? Sure. But each even number averages one point higher than each odd number. That's easy to visualize because if you begin with the number 1, then 2 is one greater. Next, 4 is one greater than 3, 6 is one greater than 5, and so forth until 80 is one greater than 79.

So? Is this a big edge or a small edge? I ran 10,000 games through my computer to find out. But even before running the program, some things were apparent. Simple mathematics told me that after all 20 keno numbers were chosen the *average* odd score would be 400 and the *average* even score would be 410.

That being the case, it would be easy to establish an over/under bet at 810. If the game ended 510 to 306 in favor of odd, then the cumulative of both scores would be 816 and those who bet over would win. Since there aren't the same variables that exist in football (such as weather conditions and injuries), I would urge the casinos to be charitable in such a bet. A customary 11-10 bet, the same as in football (where the bettor wagers $1.10 for every $1 he seeks to win), would be okay — but casinos might be more generous still.

Before discussing the odd vs. even keno contest more fully, I want to suggest another concept I feel will enhance the game. Those friends who tried out my keno program "wagered" on the *escape* more than the traditional pick-the-winning-numbers. "Betting the escape" means picking a group of numbers *none of which* must appear after 20 are chosen.

For instance, my game pays 18 to 1 if you can pick 10 numbers without any on the board being lit. The true odds against it are just under 21 to 1. If you pick...

(Escaping)

Numbers Chosen	True Odds Against	My Game pays
3	1.4 to 1	6 to 5
4	2.24 to 1	2 to 1
5	3.40 to 1	3 to 1
6	5.00 to 1	4 to 1
10	20.83 to 1	18 to 1
20	842 to 1	500 to 1

As you can see, my game handles these new bets with the same stiff percentage edge that casinos enjoy with their keno tickets. If you're interested in how the actual tickets compare and what their mathematical return is, I recommend Michael Wiesenberg's article in the February 1983 issue of *Gambling Times.*

Here's the reason I think *playing the escapes* was more exciting to my friends who tried my game than the usual keno tickets: You're always the favorite to escape the next number! Instead of sudden, unexpected success, you can ease your way into a big payoff gradually, escaping one step at a time, never being the underdog on any one number. That's psychologically satisfying. And if you don't believe me, just push this through your gaming control board and you'll see.

I usually charge handsomely for my advice, but this one's on me.

Now back to the bet which could *really* revolutionize keno. That's the odds vs. the evens. For reasons already explained, the even numbers are the favorite in the cumulative war. My computer trial of 10,000 games had *even* winning 5303, *odd* winning 4682 and there were 15 ties.

The player makes an even-money wager. If he bets $100, then he will get $200 back if he wins. The rule is that the gambler can *only bet on odd.*

You might think that the player should also be allowed to wager *even* by laying the price. But this is *my* vision, and I'll tell you why I don't want the gamblers wagering both ways.

It's long been my concept that casinos need a game where all the players are on the *same side.* Imagine the warmth and spirit, the fun and electricity in a keno parlor packed with jubilant gamblers all betting the same way. It becomes a social event. They're all in it together. This new keno would grab its own following. Each game would be a friendly, festive contest. Victory would bring cheering and congratulations. Losing would be less painful because it would be a *shared* rather than a *lonely* experience.

Here we are trailing 401 to 385 after 19 numbers. Excitement grips the room. Ninety people fix their eyes on the board. Wives cling to husbands. *Any* husbands. We watch; we hardly breathe. We need an odd number and it must be at least 17 to tie. But 17 has already been chosen, so a tie is impossible. Now it comes. The board flickers. It's 31! The final score is 416 to 401 in favor of the customers who now celebrate together and, emotionally bolstered, rush to place their next bets.

The only drawback to the casino is that the bets are unbalanced, so the house could actually suffer short-term losses. But the great advantage is that it brings keno beyond the small-bettor league and turns it into the most exciting event in town. I urge casinos to work on this *now*. It *will* work or you can have *all* my money.

PART FOUR

The Computer Age

"Your gambler's reality will hang
topside down in a distorted,
disordered semblance of the past."

Chapter 10

A Computer That Bluffs and Giggles

Why can't computers play world class poker? Is it because they don't care about money? Do they become emotionally upset? Are they compulsive gamblers? Maybe they're just stupid.

All those reasons are wrong. It turns out the problem is with the programmers. Most of my readers are not familiar with computers, and they only understand vaguely what a programmer does. It's simple. He is nothing more than a teacher.

In that sense, a computer is only a student. The relationship between programmer and computer, then, is one of teacher-student. That's a very important concept. Computer research and computer systems are restructuring the gambling scene every month. Isn't it terrific? Already, real winning strategies have been devised for sports betting, video poker and card games using high-speed computer assistance.

More than that, computers are actually playing the games. Video poker is a computer game. The cards are dealt, the choices of the player are requested and accepted, the outcome is determined and the payoffs are made — all by the computer behind the video screen. You'd think, therefore, that the computer is pretty smart.

Actually, it's the programmer who's smart. He taught the computer to do all those things. The computer was merely a good student.

Computers do exactly what they're told. They do it very fast. If I showed you two cards off the top of a deck and asked you which was the higher ranking, you could do this quickly. Typically, it might only take a second. But even a relatively slow computer can perform the equivalent of that task several thousand times in a second. Very fast computers could do it millions of times each second!

The great benefit to gamblers is that computers can follow a set of learned instructions VERY RAPIDLY and WITHOUT MAKING AN ERROR.

Think of your computer as more than a student. Think of it as a happy, efficient slave. If you tell it exactly what to do, it will please you. If your instructions are vague, it will become confused and you will not be pleased.

Computers play pretty poor poker. Say that fast six times and see if it twists your tongue. The reason is that nobody has yet figured out a way to teach a computer how to handle all the millions of unusual and unpredictable situations that occur just when you least expect them.

I am presently working on a program that will play no-limit, heads-up Hold 'Em. That's the form of poker used to determine the world champion every year at Binion's Horseshoe Club in Las Vegas. Some of the past champions have already agreed to challenge my computer in a well-publicized promotion for real money.

It's time to make a really crazy statement. How's this? My program will beat the best poker players alive. Soon I will have taught my computer almost everything I know about poker. Then it will gobble up bankrolls — especially world class bankrolls. I'm fully aware that most of the leading computer scientists and word class players will be betting against me. So what? My program will play top-flight, aggressive poker. It will bluff a lot, and even giggle. At least, it now flashes strange victory messages of its own choosing whenever it outplays you. That's almost the same as giggling.

A lot of money will be pledged against my computer. So far, nobody's come up with an offer of sizeable investment on my side. Oh, well, maybe no one trusts a computer program with a sense of humor.

Here's how I explained a computer's poker-playing ability to my friend last week. "Tell you what, Bobby. You be the computer programmer and I'll be the computer. I realize you don't know anything about programming, but don't worry." I then explained that programming is simply giving the computer a set of precise instructions that it must then follow one after another.

These instructions, I told him, are given in code called computer *language*. There's a whole bunch of high-level computer languages. My favorite is UCSD Pascal; the most commonly used is BASIC. Your computer understands these languages and will perform a small number of simple tasks. For example, your computer can get information from elsewhere (from the keyboard or a magnetic tape or a floppy disk). It already knows how to do that when you buy it. It also knows, if you instruct it in terms it understands, how to do arithmetic and how to display messages (which can be supplied by you). More importantly, it can make decisions. If one thing is true it will take one action and if another is true it will do something else.

An important computer technique is called a loop. Loops allow the programmer to tell this computer to repeat the same task over and over until something is accomplished.

Those are just about the only tools of instruction that I made available to Bobby. Since I was pretending to be his computer, he could tell me to add, subtract, multiply and divide. He could order me to store an answer under any name so that I could make reference to it later. For instance, he could ask me to add my profit or loss from the first pot to my profit or loss from the second pot and save it under a name called RESULT. At that point, I would always know what RESULT was, even if the program went on to some unrelated task and didn't return for a very long time.

Additionally, Bobby could tell me to repeat a procedure over and over until some resolution was reached. Computers understand that sort of thing.

So, now I sat at a table with a deck of cards in front of me, pretending to be a computer and waiting to learn five-card draw.

"Pick up the deck," was Bobby's first command.

"Beep, beep," I said, which is how a computer whimpers when you gave it an improper instruction.

"What's the matter?" He seemed astonished that he had violated the rules on his very first try.

Although the computer does not engage in a direct dialog with its user, I decided to speed things up by explaining, "I don't know what a deck is." After twenty minutes of awkward attempts to describe a deck in words a computer likes to hear, Bobby gave up.

I pointed out that he could tell the computer about the 52 cards by defining them as "variables" for the computer. Each would have a rank of ace down to deuce. (In Pascal, you can actually say "Ace down to deuce." in BASIC, you can code the ranks from 1 to 13 and the suits from 1 to 4.)

It was decided that it would take too long for Bobby to get a computer to deal with a deck of cards, so we took it for granted that I (his computer) already knew what a deck was.

Then Bobby said, "Deal five cards to yourself and five to your opponent."

"Beep, beep. What does *deal* mean?" I explained that first you needed five *variables* to hold one each of the opponent's cards and five to hold one each of mine. These variables (storage areas in computer memory) required names so that we could refer to them whenever needed. Bobby decided to call them WE1, WE2, WE3, WE4, WE5, THEM1, THEM2, THEM3, THEM4, THEM5, which is perfectly all right for most advanced computer languages. More typically, a programmer would declare two "arrays" called WE and THEM, with five positions each — but I hadn't told Bobby about that option. Also, he really needed *two* variables for each card, one to hold the rank and one to hold the suit. But I elected to be reasonable and not mention this. An honest-to-god computer would not have been forgiving, however.

"Now," Bobby sighed, "The first card off the deck should become THEM1, the second card should become WE1 and so forth."

Deciding to show compassion, I didn't bother to point out that "and so forth" was not a legitimate computer instruction.

Bobby said, "Now look at your hand."

"Beep, beep. What's a hand?"

Exasperated, Bobby said, "You know what I mean. Look at WE1, WE2, WE3, WE4, and WE5."

"Okay."

"If there's at least a pair of jacks, open the damn pot!" he grumbled.

"Beep, beep. What's a pair?"

"You mean a computer doesn't know what a pair is? That's incredible! Let's see. . . If two of those cards are the same AND if they're jacks or better, then open!!!"

"Beep, beep. I can't see five variables at once. I have to do one thing at a time."

Not willing to give up yet, Bobby thought and thought. Finally, he spoke very clearly. "If WE1 is the same as WE2 or WE3 or WE4 or WE5. . . or if WE2 is the same as WE3 or WE4 or WE5. . . or if WE3 is the same as WE4 or WE5. . . or if WE4 is the same as WE5 then check to see if those two cards are coded 10 or higher."

Not too bad! From ace through deuce, Bobby was coding his cards 13 down to 1. A 10 or higher meant a jack or better. Although his formula had flaws (was I supposed to check for rank or suit?), I accepted it without beeping. A real-life computer would have done something terrible here — in computer jargon, it would have crashed.

"There is no pair ranked 10 or higher," I reported.

"Then pass."

"What's pass?"

"What? I'm supposed to tell you what pass is? Okay. . . Do nothing. Just see what the opponent does."

At this point, a real opponent might communicate to the computer through the keyboard, announcing his open or pass. Bobby and I decided that our foe would open, since his hand contained a pair of kings.

"You have a bad hand. Pass," he told me.

So I sat there until he grew irritated and barked, "I said pass!"

"I am passing," I argued. "You told me pass meant to do nothing and see what the opponent does."

Deciding that a complete formula for teaching a computer poker — even with a very flexible human posing as a computer — would take a great deal of time and effort, Bobby surrendered. He asked me for a critique.

I explained that he must never assume the computer knows ANYTHING. He had forgotten to tell me what "open" meant. Instead of ordering *if I had jacks or better, THEN open,* he should have said, THEN subtract 20 units (or whatever the bet limit) from a variable called BANKROLL and add 20 units to a variable called POT. Also, he let the computer forget to ante.

Of course, his comparisons aimed at finding a pair of jacks or better were incorrect. A computer could have held 9-8-7-6-5 (a straight), 10-10-8-8-Q (two pair), a flush or many other legal openers which would not have been detected by his formula.

But that kind of problem is easily resolved. I use programs almost daily that know the strength of poker hands, make complete evaluations and output detailed reports. It's when you begin to provide the computer with rigid rules to handle strategic situations that things get tough.

For a computer to play poker at a world class level, it must take into consideration pot size, the probability that a hand will win, the possible draws and much more. It must decide when to raise and how many times to raise. It must bluff occasionally and effectively. It must speculate, for instance, about what an opponent's two-card draw means — a pair with a kicker or three-of-a-kind. And its judgment must vary depending on the situation. More that that, the program should be able to select a profitable strategy based on this evaluation.

That's hard enough, but when you try to do this in no-limit poker, things get really complicated. You now must decide not only when to bet or raise, you must decide how *much* to bet or raise. In no-limit, the computer must worry more about getting bluffed out too often or calling too frequently.

That's why one professional has said that my computer challenge against world champion humans is "Ludicrous — a computer won't play at that level for 20 years. But don't quote me." Well, you got quoted; D.H. — you just didn't get named.

Meanwhile my heads-up computer poker project continues. In about a year, the challenge will be played out. Not only am I teaching my computer strategic excellence, I'm teaching it to be gracious. Two of its many messages are: THAT WAS A VERY NICE BLUFF, I ALMOST DIDN'T CALL and I'M SORRY I TOOK YOUR MONEY, WOULD YOU LIKE TO PLAY AGAIN?

Chapter 11

Computers and Your Bankroll

Look, nobody's going to tell you the truth about computers. If you gamble, you've got about thirty-nine months of stability left. Thirty-nine months. After that your gambler's reality will hang topside down in a distorted, disordered semblance of the past.

I really care about you. And that's why I want you to listen closely.

If you drive to your nearest jungle and stand near the fringes, what will you hear? Above that ghostly whisper of wind, beyond the intertwined pools of silence... Listen! Now it comes — a shriek, high-pitched and hideous. And the words are these: "Fear not if the computers stampede, for these will create more jobs than they replace."

You must trace this shriek to its origin. You must fight your way through the foliage until you find the source. There! The creatures are in the trees above you, hanging by their tails; and the branches are snapping. One by one these creatures crash to the rocks where you stand until only a few remain crying, "Fear not if the computers stampede...!"

People don't want to know the truth about computers. You sit helplessly at your Friday night poker game while someone, somewhere nearby is sharing his thoughts with his computer. Some night soon, he'll use the techniques he's discovered and you'll watch miserably as he steals away a hunk of your bankroll.

So what can you do?

First, here are some truths you need to swallow:

(1) Very soon computers will play strategic games of chance with a proficiency that no man can possibly equal.

(2) As computers sweep into all segments of our lives, jobs will be lost. Much more time will be available for entertainment. And gambling will be everywhere. Smart gamblers with access to computer research will prosper. Others won't stand a chance.

Eventually, there will be very few jobs and a whole herd of computers will run our lives. This is not a great tragedy, but a great promise. We are heading for a tomorrow filled with leisure hours. And gambling, the great adventure *gambling,* will be more and more a part of our lives as we have more time to spend on it.

That's why we must learn to gamble correctly.

And that's why I want you to hurry off to your computer store and make friends with a computer. I want you to lay your hands on it and touch its soul. You *must* do this. Because I give you thirty-nine months, my friend.

You *need* access to a computer. You must learn how to use one, and you must act now. I don't care what your job is, how you go about your everyday business or how little you feel a computer can help — if you do not act *now,* you will be in great jeopardy in thirty-nine months!

Should you buy a computer? You can now purchase $1,000,000 worth of computing-power for a few thousand dollars. You can take it home, plug it in and let it warm your spirit.

It's going to be your best friend. Personally, I think you should buy it. Sell your house, your stereo, your car. Do whatever it takes, but buy it.

As some of you have gathered many of my poker students have been women. I have just written a book called *Poker for Women* in which I illustrate why women have special advantages playing poker that are not available to men. These stem from an inherent sexist attitude at the poker table which allows a strong woman player using my methods to win even more than a male using the same methods. I also teach male players how to avoid falling into the sex-game traps that otherwise cost money.

On the whole, I try to treat a person's intellect without regard to gender. So what I'm about to say to you women comes straight from my heart, and you damn well better pay attention to it.

It's been my experience that some very intelligent women view computers as something alien. This is probably a cultural thing. Many women think they can escape having to deal with computers by focusing their talents on the arts and by making new inroads in business.

But, you see, tomorrow's art will spill out of computers. Tomorrow's business decisions will be made by computers. Tomorrow's music will be composed and judged for artistic merit by computers. All winning gambling systems will be created by computers.

Yes, you might have some say in guiding these computers. You might suggest and reject patterns as you compose on electronic canvases. You *might,* but finally it will not be great human artists using computers for assistance. It will be great computers who are themselves the artists. They will eventually write finer novels than we ever envisioned; and make decisions grander than our most logical moments. They will surpass us in every single important intellectual field. And there's not a damn thing we can do about it!

So, if you're a woman who thinks you can escape by abandoning the computers to the men and seeking an identity of your own, you better rethink *now.* Because the sexual discrimination of the past ain't nothin', girl, compared to what's about to happen if you don't go out *today* and make friends with a computer.

Now this applies to gamblers of both sexes. What do you suppose would happen if you lived in the Middle Ages and suddenly up comes this group of folks with nuclear bombs? You might as well surrender everything, because you don't possess the tools to put up a worthy fight.

Now, that's exactly how it is with computers. A few people are arming themselves with these great weapons, and if you don't begin to understand these machines now, you will soon lose your hopes, your pride and your bankroll without even a whimper.

It used to take many months, even years, to perfect computer programs that analyze games of chance. Now a truly great blackjack program can be written, perfected and debugged in anywhere from six hours to six days, depending on how sophisticated your needs.

If you're not familiar with the modern miracle of computers, you probably think that programs that play roulette or craps are accomplishments beyond the possible scope of your understanding.

Wrong! Using a modern computer language, this single line from one of my programs throws a pair of dice and puts the result on the screen.

FOR DICE: = 1 TO 2 DO ROLL (DICE)

Some of you who are already programming might argue that ROLL is not part of the computer language [Pascal]. You're right. ROLL is the name of a procedure which simply reads: WRITE (RANDOM MOB 6 + 1). So even if ROLL were not used, the instruction is only one line of code. RANDOM is a built-in-function.)

Here it is again:

FOR DICE: = 1 TO 2 DO ROLL (DICE)

Take a good look. That's one line of computer code. Some programs are thousands of lines working cooperatively with a power that will change the face of gambling permanently. This is why you must make friends with a computer today.

In the very near future, if you cannot read and write in the language of computers, you will be considered illiterate. You have only thirty-nine months to prepare.

PART FIVE

Gambling Tactics and Advice

"We're dealing with the soul of successful
gambling. The concept is so simple
that it's almost always overlooked."

Chapter 12

Over and Under Anything

This is about overs and unders, but first...

When I answered the phone, a peculiar gruff voice responded, "You watchin' the game?"

"Yeah. Who's this?"

"You don't know me. Did you bet Oakland? I bet Oakland, but it don't look so good right now."

What kind of accent was it? Sounded like a mixture of Boston and New Jersey.

"Can I help with anything?" I prodded.

"Naw, some guys, they asked me to call you. How you doin?"

"I'm fine."

"Me too. Maybe I got a little of that flu that's 'sposed to be comin' around."

"I'm sorry to hear that."

Five seconds of silence.

"Well, you're probably wonderin' why I called. Like I said, I got your number from these friends of yours..."

"Which friends?"

"Oh, just some of the boys. Man, did you see that pass? I hope you didn't bet Oakland!"

As a matter of fact, I hadn't bet Oakland. I'd taken Cleveland and surrendered three points, and at the moment I was feeling smug, although the feeling wouldn't last. Oakland won 14-12.

When I failed to say anything, the strange voice continued.

"Here's the deal, and you can take it or leave it, no hard feelings either way."

"Thanks."

"These fellows, they wanna start the New Year right. You know what I mean? These are all tough lowball players, and they're gonna scam a few of the games. No mechanics, just best hand and a few extra raises here and there. In other words, they're gonna keep it legal. They thought with what you know and your connections that maybe you might wanna join up. They asked me to call..."

This wasn't the first time I'd been approached. I usually play my poker in Gardena, California. There are six multi-million dollar card clubs, and a lot of precautions are taken to prevent cheating. All clubs have high-caliber television cameras, and many scoundrels have been caught on video tape.

Generally, this technology is used to catch card mechanics. ("Mechanic" is the common name for a player who illegally manipulates cards.)

But another cheating problem continues to survive despite efforts of clubs to discourage it. I'm talking about partnerships — two or more players secretly in the same game playing to each other's advantage.

So, I explained to the peculiar voice on the phone that, "I consider poker an art form. It's a perfect battle of strategy and psychology. Playing with partners would destroy the thrill. Besides, I'm one of those guys who place a high value on ethics."

"Well, like I said, they're not doin' nothin' you'd be ashamed of. Man, the stuff they do your granny could still be proud of you. Like I said, they play best hand, sometimes they save bets, sometimes they put in a little extra action. It's good for the game."

"No thanks."

"Okay. No hard feelings. Sure hope you didn't bet Oakland."

Let's get something straight.

I don't like card thieves.

And if you're a card thief, here are some things you ought to know:

(1) Playing partners *is* cheating. A lot of you guys seem to have the notion that it isn't as bad as manipulating the deck or marking the cards (some of you aren't exempt from those bad habits, either).

The simple truth is that a single player marking cards is an act of dishonor. A partnership in a poker game is a *conspiracy* of dishonor.

(2) When partners use signals to play only their best hand, they aren't simply saving themselves money; they are *stealing* money from unwary opponents. Often, instead of getting money from two players when he makes his hand, an honest player profits from only one. The other, the one he was legitimately entitled to have beaten also, has not even entered the pot.

(3) Sometimes partners trap an opponent in the middle, putting in

raise after raise, knowing that only one of them has a real powerhouse hand. Where there is no limit governing the number of raises, this can be particularly dangerous. You guys better stop it!

(4) For several months, I've carefully watched some of your partnerships in action. You're making a lot of mistakes, fellows. You don't seem to know, with any degree of certainty, when to play two hands and raise liberally and when to play only your best hand. Additionally, you're betting when you should check and checking when you should bet.

(5) Well, okay. I concede that even your clumsy, primitive efforts yield substantial profits. But I can devise much more powerful strategies in 20 minutes! Why should that bother you?

You have nothing to worry about except that, theoretically, two of my guys placed in a game against *four* of yours will wind up with all the money on the table in a computer-generated time of 37 hours and 14 minutes.

That's an interesting statement. I want you thieves to read it again. Does all this theoretical stuff bore you? Well, look between the lines, baby. Maybe you're missing something.

Announcing! This author, with the support of several major card clubs is launching the world's first *Cheater Monitoring Service*. If you know or suspect anything about unethical practices going on in poker games past or present, write: Cheater Monitoring Service, *Gambling Times,* 1018 N. Cole Ave., Hollywood, CA 90038.

If you've got a boyfriend who cheats at poker, turn him in. Turn in your friends. Best of all, turn in yourself. I'm serious.

If somewhere down the tortuous avenues of life you began cheating, start fresh now. Confess! Tell me what you've done and how you've done it.

In exchange for your promise to play clean, I will personally answer any poker question of your choice.

That's a pretty good deal. You'll feel better, and you'll get some free advice to start you on your way to an honest future.

All correspondence will remain confidential, of course.

One additional note: The major poker rooms in the Los Angeles area are the best in the world. The detection methods used are remarkably sophisticated. Overall, these establishments are the safest places an honest man can play poker. I'm particularly grateful for the support expressed by the management of these clubs.

Poker...let's keep it clean.

Back to the original topic. Here we go with one of those dry mathematical subjects. Some of you already know the difference between mean and median. If you don't here's something that comes up often when you try to make spur-of-the-moment bets.

Let's say you're at a little league baseball game with a friend who's insisted that you watch his son play. This isn't your idea of a great afternoon, but there you are in the bleachers, so you might as well make the best of it. In other words, try to get a bet down.

You are suddenly struck with an idea. Instead of betting against your friend's son's team, and maybe being handicapped because he has more information, why not bet the overs and unders.

Well, if you're an avid sports bettor, you know all about this gamble. Football, baseball and basketball games are usually accompanied by an index which, if you call your friendly bookie, you can bet either over (higher) or under (lower). You generally pay 11-10 odds for the right to do this.

A typical football over and under is 38. If both teams combine for 39 points or more, you win if you bet over. Under wins at 37 or less, and 38 is a push. A common baseball over/under is 8, pro basketball, 220.

But here you are at a little league contest. These games only go six innings, but there's usually a lot of scoring.

You offer to make an over/under wager with your friend who shrugs his shoulders noncommittally. Then he agrees, "You make the line, and I'll bet it."

You say, "I'll make the line, but you flip a coin to see which side you take."

What you've just proposed is the fairest way to make a bet when neither you nor a friend wants to get the best of it.

One player makes the line; the other flips a coin to see which side he gets. Even if the line is completely inaccurate, it's still an even bet since the man flipping the coin has an equal chance of ending up with either side.

But you run into a snag, because your "friend" says, "You make the line and I'll take my choice and lay you 11 to 10 for a hundred bucks."

Feeling that you just couldn't endure the next two hours of watching this brand of baseball without some sort of a bet, you grudgingly agree.

Now your mission is to make a line as accurate as possible, so your friend won't be able to climb all over it.

A pleasant lady comes around passing out mimeographed sheets which have the league scores for the teams that played yesterday. This is the first game of the season for the two teams you're about to watch, so it's impossible to tell how they rank. But the scores from yesterday are:

Eagles	9	Raiders	8
Troupers	28	Saints	19
Kings	13	Braves	1
Turtles	25	Snails	23
Rockets	14	Porcupines	8
Trainees	11	Lads	9

You have no choice but to assume that these results are representative of the kind of games played in that league. So what should you make the over/under?

If you're like a lot of folks, you quickly saw this solution: Combine the scores for each game so you get 17, 47, 14, 48, 22, and 20. Add these outputs together (168) and divide by the number of games (6).

Since the answer is 28, you can expect 28 runs to be scored in this game on average, providing these two teams are similar to the group of teams that played yesterday.

Your friend is watching his son practice, shouting, "Thata way to go, Freddie!" and you nudge him in the ribs to get his attention. (I always figured a stiff nudge in the ribs was the right way to treat a friend who cornered you into making a wager you weren't happy with.) He turns to you a little startled.

"Twenty-eight," you say.

"Twenty-eight what?"

"That's the over and under. I make it twenty-eight."

"Oh, okay. I go under. Thata boy, Freddie!"

Now you're tied onto a bet, and the more you think about it, the more you realize there's something wrong.

As you look at the mimeographed sheet, you notice that if you had made the same line yesterday, and your friend had bet under, he would have won four out of six bets.

So, what happened? Did you use the wrong method to make your over/under line? Yep, and it's the same method that most amateur handicappers use.

What you calculated is known as the *mean*. That's the total amount produced by all trials divided by the number of trials. In this case, the total runs divided by the number of games. The method would have been correct for a different kind of bet.

Suppose you wagered $10 per run over or under a certain output. The correct line, in that case, would have been 28 – just the way you figured.

What you really wanted to calculate, in the hypothetical little league problem, was the point at which half the games would go over and half under. Look at the list of scores again. What would the proper number be? Twenty-one. This figure, known as the *median* is the one you should always use in figuring over/under lines.

For the 1980 NFL regular football season, the mean average points per game was just over 40. But the best median for all games was 37.5 (113 out of 224 games had combined scores of 38 or more, 111 were 37 or less).

Anyway, after you make your fortune betting little league baseball, remember where you got your start.

Chapter 13

Eleven Ways to Lose Money Fast

No matter how much you've learned about the technical side of gambling, we are all emotional human beings. That means we're apt to do things from time to time that are not in our best interests.

That's why people can get hurt gambling. That's why winners sometimes lose and losers sometimes destroy themselves.

I jotted down a brief list of bad habits gamblers should try to correct. It turned out there were ten.

Then I remembered that my friend, poker player/author John Fox, had once said, "I never read a sincere list that contains 10 things or 25 things or 100 things. If it were a sincere list, then it's more likely to be a number like 9 or 23 or 103."

While I think John makes too much of this point, I certainly don't want to incur his scorn. Therefore, here are my *Eleven Ways to Lose Money Fast.*

I don't care what you've been told, even the best gamblers in the world have bad habits. So, if you find some of yours on this list, don't panic; try to improve and if you fail try again.

(1) Playing Longer When Losing. The is the worst time to play longer. Even if you're not tired, mental stress is apt to cause mistakes. Besides, there could be factors contributing to your loss that you're not aware of. If you like to play long sessions once in a while, it's much better to try to extend a win than to try to get even.

(2) Borrowing Money to Gamble. Too much pressure for some. I've seen players who absolutely *never* win on borrowed money. Maybe this applies to you and maybe it doesn't. Search your soul.

(3) Playing Hunches. Although there may be reasons why your subconscious decisions are correct, it's easy to fool yourself. Most of the time a hunch player is just out-and-out guessing and usually losing a lot of money. Try science. It's the wave of the future.

(4) Keeping an Inadequate Bankroll. Most players underestimate the size of a bankroll needed to stay in action. Especially when luck is favorable, they tend to spend too much, leaving too little cushion for the bad streaks that may follow.

(5) Lending Money. If you're the kind of player who worries a lot about the money you've lent, your game will probably be damaged. Only lend money if it feels comfortable. For some it's hard to say no. But it's easy. Just say, "Every time I lend money, I lose. I think it makes me play bad or something." That's not an excuse; it's the *truth*. You'll get very few arguments.

(6) Buying a Gambling Book. There are two reasons buying a gambling book might cost you money. First, you might buy a bad book, filled with inaccurate information. Second, you might feel that you've improved your game just by *buying* the book and start gambling more recklessly. Remember, you *do* have to study the book before you can use it. You'd be surprised how much gambling literature is purchased just to build confidence but never really read.

(7) Playing When You Know You're Being Cheated. Would you quit if you knew you were being cheated? Really? *Really?*

(8) Playing Too Big for Your Bankroll. Most players tend to risk too much of their bankrolls on a given session.

(9) Playing Too Small for Your Bankroll. Players who don't bet enough to be meaningful are apt to play below their capacities. This can mean slow destruction of a bankroll.

(10) Being Superstitious. It doesn't work. It causes some players to make decisions contrary to what logic dictates.

(11) Not Making Decisions in Advance. Here's a really critical mistake. I believe no human alive has total control of his actions at all times. That's why you should try not to make important decisions on the spur of the moment. When you're calm, comfortable and thinking rationally, decide what's in your best interest. Let's say you like to play roulette, but it keeps stealing your bankroll. If you make a decision that you will never play roulette, you can probably gather enough discipline to stick to that decision.

But what if you had to make the decision all over again every time you passed a roulette wheel! Well, you might make the right choice for a while, but sooner or later, you'd be emotionally upset or tired or irrational and you'd pass a wheel and say, "What's the difference?" That's how you'd blow your bankroll.

When you just have to make the decision once, it's easy. But if you have to re-evaluate every time you walk into a casino, then you're eventually going to get into trouble. Do you see what I'm saying?

Okay, that's my list. Here's one final word of caution: *Beware!*

PART SIX

Poker Truth

"What very powerful law determines
who will eventually win and
who will lose?"

Chapter 14

Poker: Some Things to Consider

Let me ask you a question. Suppose you're playing five-card draw, jacks or better required to open. The game is eight-handed and you open in next-to-last position (seventh seat) with a pair of kings. Now the dealer calls. You each draw three. You make kings-up.

Should you bet or check?

If you answered *bet,* you probably favor an aggressive style of poker which I frequently advocated. If you said *check,* you may tend to be cautious, particularly in borderline situations. That doesn't mean you're a bad person. Caution is often a valuable tool in poker.

In my heart, I was really hoping that you wouldn't attempt to answer the question. Poker is a science of blended psychology and mathematics. The best strategy for a given hand is not always simple to discover. Sometimes it requires weighing many things very quickly under the pressure of high-stakes combat.

Here's what your hand looks like after drawing three:

Gee, this is the sort of situation that comes up all the time, isn't it? If you knew what to do at times like this, you'd be on your way to poker stardom. Maybe I can help.

Here are the ground rules for this discussion. We're talking about Gardena poker, where a joker is included in the deck. (It counts as an ace or serves to complete a straight or a flush.) The ante is $2 per player;

bets are $10 before the draw and $20 after.

Now we get to play a game called, *"You should be more inclined to be if..."*

Get out your favorite pencil and a piece of paper. For each statement, write *"Bet"* if the information makes betting more appetizing. Otherwise, write *"Check."*

(1) Your opponent has only $15 dollars left;

(2) Your opponent would not have come in with less than a pair of aces;

(3) Your opponent will never raise with less than a full house;

(4) Your opponent bluffs a lot;

(5) Your opponent will call with a pair of queens or better;

(6) Your opponent will not call with less than aces-up;

(7) Your opponent always raises with three-of-a-kind;

(8) Your opponent will never re-raise as a bluff;

(9) Your opponent will re-raise as a bluff most of the time;

(10) Your opponent never calls unless he helps;

(11) Your opponent's wife is standing behind him;

(12) Your opponent is a timid player who calls readily but seldom takes the initiative;

(13) Your opponent makes an obvious move for his chips before you decide what to do;

(14) Your opponent is looking in the other direction, appearing distracted;

(15) Your opponent is easy to read whenever he bets;

(16) You have discarded an ace;

(17) Your opponent will buff approximately the right percentage of time if you check to him;

(18) Your opponent has looked at his three new cards and keeps staring at them while waiting for you to act;

(19) Your opponent has been losing heavily and is emotionally upset;

(20) Your opponent has just bought you a cup of coffee.

Now I'll discuss each of these points, but remember this: The list does not include the *most important* factor of all: **your image.**

Answers

1. I'll accept either *bet* or *check,* as long as your logic is correct. This was given as the first question to show that even when you've listed the factors to be weighed, you won't necessarily know on which side of the

scale to weigh them.

A player who has less than the full bet in front of him cannot raise, therefore your *bet* is safer than usual. However, he may be reluctant to call with his last money, deciding to fold unless he has at least three of a kind. This would make it better to *check,* since you'll only get called if you lose.

2. *Bet.* Players tend to call with a pair of aces against another three-card draw, especially if the bettor has a loose image. Of course, the fact that this opponent can't improve to losing hands such as queens-up weighs against your bet. Still, all things considered, this goes on the *Bet* side of the scale.

3. *Bet.* You can throw your hand away safely if you get raised.

4. *Check* with the intention of calling. Try to lure the bet if you can.

5. *Bet.* This is exactly what you're hoping for.

6. *Check.* You'd just be betting into trouble with no prospect of gain.

7. *Check.* Unless you can safely lay down your hand to raise (because your opponent has a tell or because he never bluffs), this can be an expensive bet.

8. *Bet.* You won't have to pay off a raise. This is similar to #3.

9. *Bet* with the intention of calling a raise. This very profitable play also works well against aggressive players with strong egos.

10. *Check.* Now you have no chance of being called by a lone pair of aces (or less). Being called by a pair of aces is the main reason why a borderline bet with kings-up is profitable.

11. *Check.* As discussed in my *Book of Tells,* a player is less likely to bluff or make marginal calls when a friend or relative is watching. Players fear embarrassment.

12. *Bet.* Timid players who call a lot but seldom raise are about the easiest opponents you can hope for. Bet all your marginal hands into this breed.

13. *Bet.* Again from the *Book of Tells* we know that this is normally an act intended to keep us from betting.

14. *Check.* Another tell. This player has helped his hand and will bet. Your two-step strategy is simple: 1) Check; 2) Pass when your opponent bets.

15. *Check.* Maybe he'll bet and then you'll know exactly what to do.

16. *Bet.* Especially if your opponent is likely to begin with aces. The fact that you discarded an ace makes it harder for him to make trips.

That means you're less likely to be raised and, therefore, your bet is safer.

17. *Bet.* If your opponent bets the appropriate amount of times from a game-theory standpoint, you will not be able to profit after checking. (In fact, you'll lose money because correct strategy here dictates that you call most of the time and *lose* most of the time! An exception would be if this opponent frequently began with less than aces and often bet two small pairs. Then you'd win a larger than normal share by calling.)

Anyway, you might as well seize the initiative and *bet,* provided you have reasonable chances of being called by an inferior hand. If your opponent will frequently fold aces-up (which isn't likely), you might even consider betting for *that* reason.

18. *Bet.* A classic tell. He doesn't have anything worth staring at: It's just an act. Fire into him!

19. *Bet.* Emotionally damaged poker players typically call everything that moves.

20. *Check.* Players who feel they've befriended you won't make marginal calls. Therefore you have nothing to gain by betting, unless you can get aces-up to fold — which is almost impossible in limit poker.

What was this lesson about? How to play kings-up? No.

My message is: Be aware of as many things about an opponent as you can. Everything you analyze will make your bet, call or raise either more or less favorable. Some things are very important, others have almost no bearing, but *everything* you consider helps at least a little.

My list did not include all that should be contemplated. In fact, the list did not necessarily contain the most important things. It was merely an example of how disciplined thought can help you make the winning choices.

The most important factor governing whether or not you should bet a marginal hand is how your opponent feels about *you.* If he considers you wild, crazy and bizarre, he's more likely to call. If he thinks you're conservative, your marginal bets will be wasted, but you can successfully bluff more often.

There are four main images I use in a poker game: crazy, angry, drunk, and professional. In some future book, I'll explain each of these in detail. The art of conveying the right impression is very important in the poker universe. Several articles and poker books mention no-win advertising plays I've supposedly attempted. A lot of these stories are exaggerated.

Nevertheless, *crazy* and *erratic* is usually the thing to strive for in a limit game. Your opponents find it very intimidating when they can't figure out what's coming next. I have, by actual study, determined that nothing surpasses the hourly profit of a good crazy image.

So, if you ask me, sanity doesn't make sense.

Chapter 15

The Law of Least Tilt

Is it the **Law of Averages?**
Certainly not! Well, surely it isn't the Law of Diminishing Marginal Utility. That's right, it isn't. The Law of Gravitation, perhaps? No.
How about the Law of the Jungle? Funny, guess again! Did I hear you wager that it's the Law of Excluded Middle? Well, just how much do you want to bet? That isn't even close, and I can't fathom why you said it. Come on, make a REASONABLE guess this time.
Oh, I see. You're tired of guessing because you don't know what the question is. Okay, I'll repeat it:
"In a poker game among eight equally matched world class players, what very powerful law dictates who will eventually win and who will lose?"
You're thinking, "Who cares? How often am I in a poker game made up of eight equally matched world class players?"
Ah, but this principle has a much broader importance. It ranks among the most powerful laws in the gambling universe. Great poker pros are governed by it. So are Henry, Jack and Felix at your Friday night game. So are blackjack players and golfers, craps shooters and backgammon superstars.
I'm talking about *The Power*, baby. It's a black hole in the poker table that can suck up all your chips and send you home whimpering. I'm talking about a merciless, ubiquitous, universal law that will never leave you alone until you honor it.
I'm talking about *Caro's Law of Least Tilt*.
Exactly what is tilt, anyway?
You might not know the meaning of the phrase "going on tilt." Turning to the *Random House Dictionary of the English Language* (unabridged), we find on page 606 that "going on tilt" is not defined.
A pity. But checking a more credible source, Doyle Brunson's *Super/System — A Course in Power Poker*, we see that the term "on

tilt" is defined on page 539. Quote: "When a player starts playing bad (loses his composure), usually after losing one or more big pots, he's said to be *on tilt.*"

There are other slang ways to express this phenomenon. Vegas regulars call it "steaming." In my favorite Denver game, we used to say a man had "flipped a pancake."

Going on tilt describes it best. What happens to a pinball machine when you shake it too hard? The lights go out, its normal mechanical functions are short-circuited, it stops playing its normal game, and suddenly the word *Tilt* flashes on its scoreboard.

Isn't that what happens to a poker player when you shake him too hard? Most players can take their bad beats graciously for a while; but when they suffer one blow too many, something usually snaps. Their lights go out, their brains malfunction, they cease to play their best game and, if you look really close, you can see the word *Tilt* etched on their foreheads.

Suddenly the most dedicated scientific poker players are babbling and bluffing and barging into pots with inferior hands. You've seen it happen, and it's a pitiful sight to behold.

Write this law on a piece of paper, tape it to the wall and study it. Caro's Law of Least Tilt: *Among similarly skilled opponents, the player with the most discipline is the favorite.*

Gee, that seems too obvious to bother saying. Obvious, hell! Ask around and see what the best poker players think is most important. Their opinions will vary. To save you the trouble, I actually surveyed ten tough players. My question was: "In a poker game among players whose ability is about equal, what do you think is the most important winning edge?"

Using a little judgement, I placed their answers into the following categories—

Knowledge of mathematics: 4
Psychological skill: 3
Knowing when to quit: 2
Alertness: 1

Had I undertaken a larger survey, other things would have appeared. But the point is made by this small sample. Incredibly, nobody mentioned the Law of Least Tilt! Everything listed *is* important.

Knowledge of Mathematics. A very weak player who knows nothing about probabilities or mathematics will be at the mercy of a knowledgeable opponent. However, a player with an *outstanding* grasp of odds and statistics is only a small favorite over a player with a *pretty good* understanding.

Of course, in some poker games even a small difference in mathematical ability can be critical. Seven-card high-low split is such a game.

Psychological Skill. Very important. But, in a game involving contestants of equal overall talent, is it likely that there will be much difference here? No.

Knowing When to Quit. For a bunch of reasons which I don't want to discuss now, it's better to quit when you're losing than when you're winning. Most players get this backwards and play longer when they're losing. Anyway, seldom does one player secure an important edge over his peers by quitting at the correct times.

Alertness. You'll seldom find a game among equally skilled foes where one is substantially more alert than his opponents.

Tour the card rooms of Las Vegas, the poker parlors of California, the private games in Texas. Try legal seven-stud in Washington and Oregon. Play Hold 'em in Montana.

Yep, poker's booming everywhere. Look for the toughest, meanest game in the area. Ask around, you'll find it. It's usually a medium or high-stakes contest and it's often comprised of the same regular players night after night. Sometimes there's a stranger to throw off some money; but usually it's survival of the fittest—hometown heroes battling for regional honors.

I'm talking about a poker game where men of approximately the same expectations wage a war of egos. Listen to me, you seven-stud superstars at the Sahara — I'm talking to you!

Almost every ego contest I've witnessed has an unspoken rule that goes like this: *Weak players are timid and we're not weak, so let's bet our hands like crazy. Nobody will get hurt if everyone does it.*

There's more to this tacit understanding. *Any player who suffers two bad beats in a row is expected to play more recklessly than usual.*

Oh, I almost forgot, there's another part. *If a stranger gets in the game and tries to take advantage of our generous bets and raises, we'll play conservatively.*

This last part is consistently violated. Take these poker pros and near-pros aside and ask what they'd do if a solid, talented player from Milwaukee sat in their game.

"We don't *give* action unless we *get* action." Snail slime!

The sad thing is, these guys really believe this! Gosh, you take your skilled seven-stud player from Topeka and put him in the $30 and $60 limit seven-stud game at the Sahara and . . . well, I like his chances.

The talent in this game is awesome. Gathered here at the Sahara is some of the keenest seven-stud talent that ever sprouted West of the Rockies. But, yes they *do* play too recklessly and when they lose too many pots and get on tilt they play *really* recklessly.

Naturally, you'd expect this to stop when Fred from Sacramento sits in the game. You guys remember Fred, don't you? Following my instructions he won $3210 in one session. You probably don't remember, since that isn't a milestone win. And, of course, you don't remember Charlie since he won only $1530.

These players were sent in the game as an experiment; and they both reported the same thing. The regular players did *not* lighten up on their raises. Instead, they made these new players a target and tried to intimidate them with a barrage of irrational raises.

Following my advice, both Fred and Charlie called timidly for the first several pots, letting the aggressors establish an image. Then they counterattacked for three consecutive hands. They'd been instructed to get the last bet in at every opportunity (within reason) no matter what cards they held. Although Charlie managed to lose all three pots, Fred won two of his, once making an inside straight down the river against queens-up.

According to plan, Fred and Charlie never got out of line after that. They had established an early reckless image. The image stuck, even though they played solid poker from then on. The regular players felt confident that the tacit loose-play agreement was not in jeopardy. No one, they reasoned, was taking advantage.

Although these two sessions are not significant enough to prove the point, let's make believe they are. What the hell, we're talking about more than 400 hands, and only a statistician would demand a larger sample.

What it proves is this: *In a game where everyone goes "on tilt" some of the time, the player who spends the fewest minutes "on tilt" wins the most money.*

(Since some tilt plays are horrible and others are merely bad, you could argue that it isn't the time of tilt, but the quality of tilt that determines the winners. It's really both.)

Controlled Tilt is simply doing the things that a player "on tilt" does, while being motivated rationally rather than emotionally. The strategy is to appear totally berserk while remaining thoroughly in command. This is the cruelest, most profitable tactic I know.

PART SEVEN

Crash Courses in Poker

"You will win because the advice is
enough to snare mountains of
chips."

Chapter 16

Seven-Card Stud: A Crash Course

Only 11% of adult American males, ages 21 to 70, have ever read a poker book. Surprised? Well, that figure isn't based on some statistical study using error-prone sampling methods; rather, it is derived from an actual rough estimate.

To most folks, poker is casual entertainment, played for reasonable stakes. The average guy is too involved with his own problems to invest hundreds of hours mastering the very technical strategy and mathematics that relate to world class poker. What busy people need are simple poker formulas that work.

Wouldn't it be terrific if you could stride proudly into a Las Vegas casino, sit at a $1-to-$4 limit seven-stud table and destroy the game in an hour or two? If you only knew the correct strategy for small-limit seven-stud, you could vacation in Las Vegas any time you felt like it, and it wouldn't cost anything. In fact, you'd make money — modest wins of $50 to $300 on average. Unfortunately, you don't know the formula. Too bad.

A couple of months ago, I phoned *Gambling Times* editor Len Miller. "How are you, my boy?" he greeted in his typical amiable manner. I explained that I'd been trying to distill the various popular forms of poker into easy-to-learn guidelines that anyone could master in a matter of minutes.

I explained, "I'm going to simplify different poker games now and then. The formulas will be strong enough that even a novice should win consistently at small and medium-limit games. Instead of wasting lots of time explaining technical stuff, I'll cut corners in order to present the best-fit strategy that will cover the majority of situations."

"Good!" enthused Len. "I think you should begin with seven-stud since that's the most popular poker game in America."

So here it is, folks, the first of capsulized poker strategies. Remember, this is a crash course in seven-stud. That means the advice was sort of "smoothed out" and sometimes it doesn't provide the optimum strategy for an exact situation. Even so, you'll win nicely overall. You have my promise.

Although the formula given is aimed specifically at the $1-to-$4 limit game, it works great for similar ranges such as $1-to-$3. The concepts can be readily adapted to larger limits, like $5 and $10. Also these principles work well for home poker games.

If you don't have any use for this seven-stud lesson, then go away. You can spend this time doing something else. If you've never read Steinbeck's *Grapes of Wrath,* I recommend it.

You and I owe a really massive amount of thanks to a guy named Rick Greider. Although Rick has quietly remained out of the poker spotlight, most big-name players respect him as a tremendous talent.

But hardly anyone knows this: For the past two years, Rick has averaged five hours a day *away* from the poker tables working on seven-stud. He has labored both on his own and in cooperation with computer programmers running high-speed simulations.

Rick Greider is the world's top authority on seven-stud. That's a tribute to someone who never got his fair share of recognition.

After I formulated my guidelines for small-limit seven-stud, Rick agreed to go over these point-by-point, making some additions and modifications. Although our strategy makes many compromises for the sake of simplicity and is definitely not intended for a high-stakes game against accomplished opponents, we both sincerely believe that if you use this method, you must win.

Here's a description of the specific game this formula is suited to, although the advice is also applicable to other seven-stud games.

The limit is $1 to $4, which means a player has an option of betting or raising in amounts of $1, $2, $3, or $4. Just as in your normal home-variety seven-stud, the players are each dealt three cards, two down, one up. In most Vegas card rooms, the lowest card is "forced" to make an initial token wager of half a dollar (called "bringing it in"). This comes in addition to a dime ante. The lowest card "brings it in" because that is thought to stimulate action.

There are two frequent variations. One is no ante. The other, high card brings it in. If either of these rules applies, you should play somewhat less liberally.

There are betting rounds after the third, fourth, fifth, sixth and seventh cards. The last card is dealt face down. If you raise on any given round, that raise must at least equal the amount of the bet. In seven-stud you select the best five-card hand from among your seven cards, normal ranking of poker hands applying.

I'll be using the term "street" in this chapter. That's simply the conventional way of describing how many cards have been dealt to each contestant so far. The first betting round is on third street, the last on seventh street. Ready?

Many times a casino will have more than one $1-to-$4 limit game. You might watch these games for a few minutes. The ideal choice for this strategy is the one with the most players per pot with a minimum amount of raises. That's because, in *any* kind of poker, you'll make the most money against timid opponents who call with weak hands but don't get maximum value out of their strong hands.

Don't worry about the competition being too tough. You'll almost never find sophisticated players at this level. They're just there to have fun and give away a little money. Might as well take it, don't you think? Go ahead and sit down.

In terms of profit, whether you play your first three cards or not is the mcst critical decision you'll need to make. These are the important considerations:

(1) The strength of your hand.

(2) How many players are yet to act behind you. (The more there are, the more vulnerable your hand is.)

(3) The exposed (up cards) of your opponents.

Of course, there are other factors as well, such as how much it will cost to call and how many other players are active. But our formula ignores these aspects. For instance, if you think you have the best pair, raise no matter what. If you have a large three-flush, call for up to $2.

Starting requirements filter down to this: If you have better than three jacks, an ace-high three-flush or three parts of a straight flush, just call and try to keep players in. If you have trips smaller than jacks or the probable best pair, raise and chase players out.

Examples: With these starting hands, you should raise and chase players out...

(Of course, you might not even play the pair of queens or the pair of tens. If you do, raise.)

With these starting hands, you should just call and keep players in...

Got it? If you do that and the rest of your game is just average, you're already doing well enough to make money against weak competition!

If you hold this set of trips or higher...

you should simply call whatever the bet is on third street, even if it's only 50 cents. Wait until fourth street, then bet $4 every chance you get, unless you feel someone has a better hand. Don't expect to start with a hand this good very often. The odds against it are 1,380 to 1.

With a lesser three-of-a-kind, raise $2 if the bet is only 50 cents. If someone has already made it more than 50 cents, raise $4.

Play a pair of aces and kings the same way.

Now we come to the tricky stuff—pairs less than kings. If a king in an early position bets, say $2 and you have Q-Q-2, *throw it away! Don't ever play a pair of queens or less if a player shows strength by betting with a higher card.*

You should keep in mind that if your opponent does have a pair on his first three cards, two out of three times it will be of the exposed denomination. Therefore, usually *assume a bettor has a pair of his door card* (the exposed card). However, common sense suggests that if an opponent bets with a three showing, he's unlikely to have merely a pair of threes.

Don't play pairs smaller than tens against more than one opponent. With any pair on third street, either raise or throw your hand away.

Rick defines the key to winning as "isolating your pair head-up against an opponent with a lesser pair." That's true of all forms of seven-stud. When you have a pair, try to raise players out — you don't want three-way action!

Here are four other typical hands you might consider starting with...

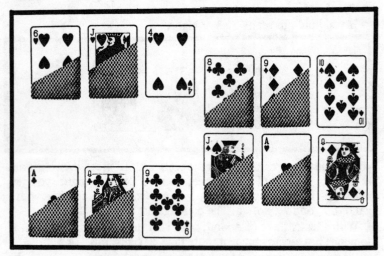

These are "come" hands, which means they can potentially become a straight or a flush. If it's only 50 cents and no one behind you is apt to raise, call with any of these. Otherwise *only* play the three clubs. Even then, don't come in if it costs more than $2.50 (the original 50 cents plus a $2 raise).

Although the 8-9-10 may look tempting, and most large-limit players call small bets to see a fourth card, these hands are very big losers in small-limit games: here a large number of players compete for the pot and the average winning hand is abnormally strong.

Simply stated: On your first three cards, *never call for more than half a dollar with any come hand except a straight flush or a flush that includes an ace.*

In general, when you have one pair and it looks like the best hand, you must try to get head-up against an opponent. This is mandatory! Never (NEVER!) slow play ANY pair in small-limit seven-stud.

If you have any question about whether yours figures to be the best pair, throw it away. Pay attention to the other players' door cards. Remember, it's not just the strength of your hand that's important. It's your hand in relation to your opponents' hands. Not only do the exposed cards give you an idea of what other players are betting, they often indicate whether or not you should play.

For example, seldom invest money on a pair of queens if someone has a queen for a door card. Don't ever play *any* three-card flush if two or more of your suit are showing.

Is that simple enough? Well, that was the tough part. After third street, the rest is easy. Here are some important tips:

If an opponent has put in any action above the token 50-cent opening bet, he's usually going "to the river" (seventh street). Once a player has committed himself on third street, it's going to take more than a maximum $4 bet to scare him out.

Maybe that sounds like bad poker, but usually you *also* will be going to the river once you put anything more than 50 cents into the pot on third street. That's why the play-or-not-play decision is so vitally important.

Here are two situations where you *should* throw your hand away:

(1) A player bets on fourth street or fifth street after pairing his door card. (Fold one pair or two pair.)

(2) A player, who's been just calling, catches a third suited card on fifth street and bets. (Fold any pair, including aces, and any potential straight or small flush. If you're playing properly, it's unlikely that you have a small come hand at this point, unless you began with a possible straight flush.)

Don't pay for a fifth card unless you're prepared to take a seventh card! In other words, it will require a rare event for you to throw away your hand on sixth or seventh street.

Your style of play should be straightforward. That is, don't try to be tricky. Your opponents, at this level of play, will call anyway. Sandbagging (checking and then raising) is out! Do you understand what I'm telling you? It's important. *Don't sandbag.*

Also, *don't bluff!* This advice is absolutely essential in a small-limit casino game. (It's true of home poker games as well. Strong players are particularly vulnerable to making this mistake. When you're against a lineup of pleasure players, forget about bluffing.) You can occasionally try to steal the ante and the "bring in" bet if you're *last to act.* Raise $1. If you get called, give it up—that is, don't bet on fourth street and, if you get bet into, pass.

If your ego demands that you play a clever game, the $1-to-$4 limit is not the right arena to show off. As Rick puts it, "Tight is right in the one-to-four limit."

Chapter 17

Five-Card Draw: A Crash Course

Look, I didn't want to write about draw poker. I've got other stuff on my mind.

Here's an example. A month ago I was at a party and this medium-young woman said, "Poker? I could never play poker. I don't believe in competition."

So I asked (these weren't my exact words, but they're as close as I can remember), "Okay, medium-young woman, tell me why you don't like competition."

"Because I believe in cooperation."

Didn't that nonsense die out five or six years ago? Guess not. For a while, people were teaching their kids not to compete. Games faded from fashion. Too bad. Nobody gets very good at anything that way. You see, competition is an agreed upon endeavor. The result is that everyone grows stronger!

Competition and cooperation are not opposites. They are both powerful concepts, but they exist in harmony. There *is* no competition without cooperation.

This subject isn't meaningless and abstract. It is of particular importance to gamblers.

But now, I've got to keep my promise. I said I would talk about five-card draw poker. Elementary ethics dictate that I deliver.

This is the second in a series of crash courses on various forms of poker. You are forbidden to take this course until you understand the following:

This is *not* a discussion of sophisticated techniques. Complicated plays, ploys and probabilities have been omitted. These guidelines have been smoothed out — that is, the advice has been tailored to fit a wide range of situations in a highly profitable way. There are situations where use of this advice will be wrong, but, even so, if you stubbornly use this method without variation, you *must* win in the small-limit game for which it is intended.

119

What's the purpose of these quick courses? To teach an inexperienced player some easy-to-understand standards which he can learn in *minutes.*

No attempt is made to provide advice for everything you might encounter in a poker game. What if you make a very high flush and the opener, who stood pat, bets into you — call or raise? When should you bet three-of-a-kind into a three-card draw? How many raises should you go with a pat straight flush?

Answers to questions such as these are not supplied. The presumption is that you'll use your own best judgement and that it will be at least equal to the judgement of your unsophisticated opponents. Sometimes you'll make the wrong play, but so will they. It evens out.

You will win because the advice given is, in itself, enough to snare mountains of chips against weak-to-moderate opposition.

Although many of the guidelines you're about to learn work well for home games, and they're even useful for a 52-card deck without a joker, this discussion deals with the game as it's played in Gardena, California.

Does everyone know about Gardena? Some say it's the Poker Capital of the World. That's a snappy title, and there's good justification for it. Its population is only 47,000, but there are six legal poker clubs. These are classy establishments with 35 tables each. Only 20 freeway minutes from Gardena is the city of Bell where the new California Bell Club boasts 67 tables.

Until the Bell Club opened, Gardena did little advertising, so the facilities were largely unknown, even to poker players in the Los Angeles area.

To be sure, there are large and small cardrooms throughout California — all devoted to five-card draw poker (either standard or lowball), and all legal. But Gardena, with upwards of 100 tables in action 'round the clock, is poker paradise.

Our target game for this course is $2/$4 limit draw poker. You can walk right in and sit down at this game. Using the formula that comes next, you'll begin making money immediately. Later, you'll be able to add your own strategies and finesses.

A friend who's written a poker book once confided, "You can't just take someone off the street and teach him to beat draw poker."

Sounds reasonable, John. But I can. And here is that formula, which should take all of 15 minutes to learn.

First let's get the rules straight. There are eight players per table. Each deals in turn. The ante is 25 cents. Before the draw all bets are $2. A pair of jacks or better is required to open. You can draw as many cards as you wish, up to five.

After the draw, all bets and raises are $4. Occasionally no one will open. Then there's another quarter ante and the stakes become $3 before the draw and $6 after. If the pot still isn't opened, a third quarter is anted, making the total 75 cents per player, and the betting becomes $4/$8.

Got it?

Choose a table. The best is one where there are a lot of players per pot and everyone seems to be having a good time.

Look at your first hand. Remember, it takes jacks or better to open. Your hands will only be that good 22.4% of the time.

(I'll be referring to seating position throughout this text. The player immediately to the left of the dealer is in position one. To the left of position one is position two, and so forth. The dealer, if the game is eight-handed, is in position eight. The order of action is clockwise.)

Okay, you're only going to get openers about twice in nine deals. Suppose you're in first position with this hand.

Not only do you have openers, but you hold a pair considerably better than plain old jacks. In fact, you'll only get a hand this good about one time in six. Your pulse rises. You clear your throat. Excitedly, your hands reach for your chips as you prepare to open.

DON'T DO IT!

Are you nuts? You can't open with kings in first position! I guess I'll just have to give you a chart so you know what to open with. Here:

Position	Minimum Openers
1	Aces, no two pair except aces-up
2	Aces, no two pair except aces-up
3	Aces, no two pair smaller than queens-up
4	Aces, no two pair smaller than queens-up
5	Aces or better (includes ANY two pair)
6	Kings
7	Queens
8	Jacks

Memorize that. Those of you familiar with some of my other writings on poker will complain that this advice is different from my usual suggested strategy. That's because I wanted to present these standards in a simple form that is easy to memorize.

Notice that you can always open with aces. Because a pair of aces is a relatively common hand, occurring once every 21 deals, you'll make more money with them than with any other category of hand. Also note that a small pair should not open from the early positions.

The mathematics of the phenomenon are complex, but they basically center on the fact that it's a lot harder to help two pair (8.3% chance of improvement) than a pair of aces (as much as 37% chance of improvement if it's an ace-joker combination).

I'm instructing you to open exactly as the chart dictates without grumbling.

All right, pretend you had that pair of kings in first position. You felt the urge to open, but the chart forbade such action. So you passed, and the dealer opened.

Now you've got him, right? You showed discretion by not opening, because you didn't want to risk getting raised. You patiently waited for someone else to open. You're in luck; that patience has been rewarded.

It's up to you to act. You grab your chips. The idea of raising the opener occurs to you. After all, he's in last position. Everyone else has passed, so he's likely to come barging into the pot with merely a pair of jacks, right? But the chips feel heavy in your hand, and you decide to merely call.

WAIT!

What the hell do you think you're doing? Do you want to lose the grocery money? You can't call with a pair of kings — EVER!

Well, all right, here's a chart that explains what you should call with, depending on the opener's position:

Position of Opener	Minimum Calling Hand
1	Queens-up
2	Queens-up
3	Aces, no two pair smaller than jacks-up
4	Aces, no two pair smaller than jacks-up
5	Aces
6	Aces
7	Aces
8	Aces

As you can see, unless you have at least a pair of aces, you must never call an opener (with the exception of some "come hands" discussed later). Also, two weak pair are unplayable against an early-position opener.

If you do specifically what these previous two charts say, you will already be making money in the target game — the $2/$4 limit in Gardena.

Just by following those instructions, you will be avoiding the two most costly mistakes made in draw poker. One is to open with weak hands in early positions. The other is to call with jacks, queens or kings.

Often you'll have a hand which you could convert into a straight or flush by drawing one card. Some of these hands should be played, and others shouldn't.

This is a country straight:

There are nine cards that will turn this into a straight. These are the cards:

Unfortunately, there are 39 cards that won't help (assuming you threw away a deuce). That's 4.3 to 1 against, and the possibility of getting this hand beaten, even if you do make it, means it's *never playable*.

Here are two four-flush draws:

The first hand should not be played. The second is worth calling an unraised pot if there are two or more opponents already involved. The rule is that a four-flush must never be drawn to unless it includes an ace.

The joker presents other unusual drawing problems. Here's a 12-way straight (12 cards can complete it):

It can be played any time you would play a four-flush with an ace. Here's a better hand, a 16-way straight:

If the pot isn't raised, you can always call with the hand above. There are hands with even more than 16 cards that will help them. These straight-flush draws are pretty rare and, for the sake of simplicity, they should be played just like 16-way straights.

If a pot is opened, what should you raise with?

Most of your opponents at this level of play will raise with aces-up or better no matter what the position of the opener. This, it turns out, is a pretty good strategy. Use it.

If the pot is already raised, you should come in "cold" (for two bets) with three eights or better. If you have three fives, pass.

If you open and get raised, you should fold with jacks, queens, kings and any two pair smaller than Aces-up. Although it's correct mathematically to throw away aces in this circumstance, it's better for your table image to call.

Stick to the formula.

In Gardena there's a herd of little old pensioners who walk around mumbling, "Never bet into a one-card draw." It seems to be the only thing on their minds.

How did you last so many years in Gardena? "I never bet into a one-card draw."

Been winning lately? "Nope. Not since last month. Can't understand it, either — I haven't been betting into one-card draws."

Although you're learning a *simple* winning formula, there is one finesse I'm going to teach you. If you hold three-of-a-kind after the draw against an opponent who's drawn one, always bet unless you're sure he's on the come.

Another play that involves a bit of sophistication is sandbagging (checking and then raising). You won't be doing a lot of it, even though the $2/$4 limit draw with a 25-cent ante is an ideal format for this technique.

This is a checklist for sandbagging:

(1) There are at least five players still to act behind you;

(2) Your hand is three deuces or better;

(3) There is no jack, queen, king, ace or joker in your hand.

Always sandbag if all three of those conditions are true. Otherwise never sandbag.

All the following hands can be sandbagged if at least five players are yet to act:

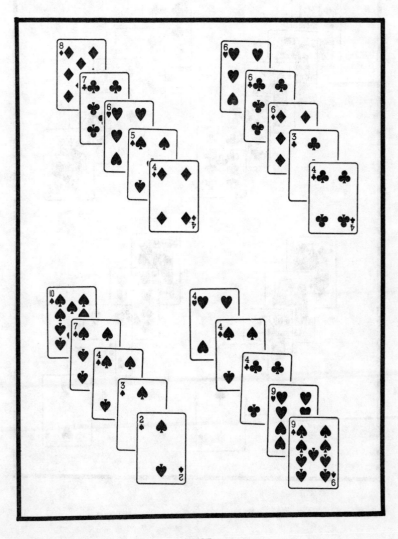

These hands can never be sandbagged:

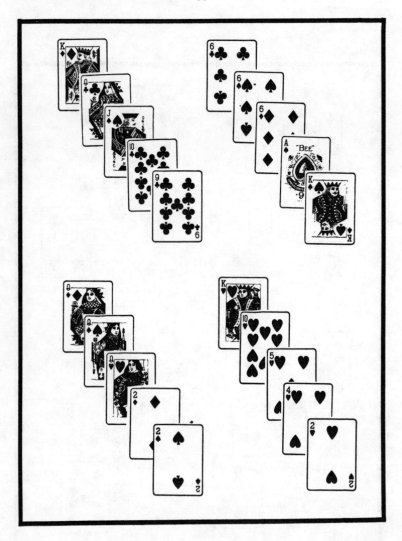

The reason you don't want to sandbag jacks, queens, kings, aces or the joker is that, by existing in your hand, these cards are denied to an opponent. And these are precisely the cards that will help an opponent open. Remember, your sandbag cannot succeed unless someone opens.

I've got to say this once more, because I'm sorta afraid it didn't sink in. This is *not* a sophisticated course on draw poker.

You now possess a five-draw emergency kit. It permits you to set foot in the poker capital of the world — Gardena — and win real, spendable money, even if you never heard of the place before.

Not only that, if you follow this advice exactly, you will be the best at your table the very first time you play!

Thank you, Mike.

Chapter 18

Lowball Draw: A Crash Course

There's an overworked adage that goes, "Lowball isn't a game; it's a disease."

In most public cardrooms, they provide a separate section for low poker. That's because lowball players are very sick human beings. And because of that, management has decided that the beasts of lowball should not mingle with the gentlemen of jacks-or-better.

As a group, lowball addicts tend to be irritable and unmannerly. They didn't start out that way. It took years and years of drawing one card to a seven and missing 72.9% of the time to create these cranky creatures.

Lowball is a series of predictable frustrations. Bad things happen to your hands *most of the time!* In standard draw poker (highball), if you draw two to this hand:

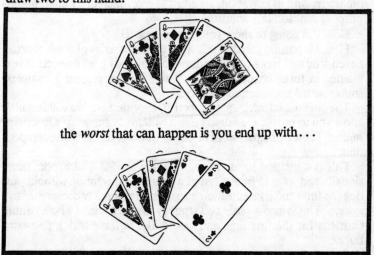

the *worst* that can happen is you end up with...

To put it simply, you can't hurt your hand. You begin with an excellent combination, and you retain that original strength while taking a *free* shot at improving. All in all, drawing can be a *comfortable* experience in jacks-or-better poker.

What about lowball? Let's say you have this hand:

You're looking at a pat ten-high. But you're also looking at the best possible draw in the universe! In all probability you'll decide to draw a card. Unfortunately, 43.8% of the time you're fated to finish with a hand *worse than what you started with!*

That doesn't seem fair!

Lowball is a battle among ill-natured opponents who whine and whimper, sulk and snarl. It is an angry competition spiced with animosity and aggravation. Its spirit is cold, incredibly cold, and its purpose is absolutely nonproductive.

Now I'm going to show you how to beat it!

First, I'll remind you that this is the third in a series of crash courses. Seven-stud and jacks-or-better draw have already been covered. As explained in those chapters, these courses do not present a complex, sophisticated approach to winning.

The purpose is to present a powerful, *easy* method that will *instantly* allow you to profit. *Do not use this technique in games of $20 limit or higher.* These principles work best against weak-to-moderate competition.

This is a method to use if you're going to visit a cardroom occasionally and want to be assured of a winning expectation without putting the time and concentration into mastering a really comprehensive system. This is also a very good strategy to give a friend who's visiting Gardena for the first time and would like to leave with a few extra bucks.

As in all these crash courses, the advice has been "smoothed out." That means that the general strategy might be slightly *wrong* for a few situations that arise, but will be overwhelmingly *correct* for most situations. All in all, this strategy has been thoroughly tested and *will win.*

Professional-level lowball strategies, such as my four-page *Advanced Strategy* or the section included in Doyle Brunson's *Super/System*, are exceptionally powerful and I recommend them to serious students.

If you've ever wondered how rare certain lowball hands are compared to high hands, this chapter should help you. I'm often asked questions like, "Is it harder to get a pat seven in lowball than a pat flush in high?"

The accompanying *before the draw* matchups show a high hand (left) that is approximately as rare as the lowball hand (right). In the first case, we see that a wheel is about as hard to get pat as queens-full or better. (Calculations are for a deck that includes a joker, which is pretty standard nowadays.)

Yes! Being dealt a pat seven-high straight or *higher* is equivalent to getting a pat seven or *lower* — and that makes for good conversation.

It's also interesting that in lowball (53-card deck) a pat 8-4 (1400-1) is harder to get than a pat bicycle (1245-1). You can dazzle your grandma with that fact!

Lowball draw is pretty popular in America. Most social scientists place it between Denver Omelettes and pedigree kittens on a popularity scale.

In Gardena, California (and neighboring Bell), where the game is legal and played publicly, the rules go like this:

(1) The best hand you can get is 5-4-3-2-A of any suit;

(2) Ace is the *lowest* (meaning best) card;

(3) Straights and flushes don't count against you — forget they exist;

(4) The limit after the draw is *double* the limit before the draw;

(5) Usually everyone antes and, additionally, the player to the left of the dealer puts in a *blind* bet (he *must* open the pot no matter what cards he has);

(6) You can draw any number of cards from zero to five;

(7) A joker is included in the deck, and it becomes whatever card would make your hand lowest. If you have 8-4-3-2-joker, the joker is an ace. With 6-5-2-A-joker, it's a 3.

The object, remember, is to end up with the lowest hand. 5-4-3-2-A beats 6-5-4-3-2. K-7-4-3-2 beats 6-3-2-A-A (pair of aces). *But* 6-3-2-A-A beats 5-4-2-2-A (pair of deuces, aces are low).

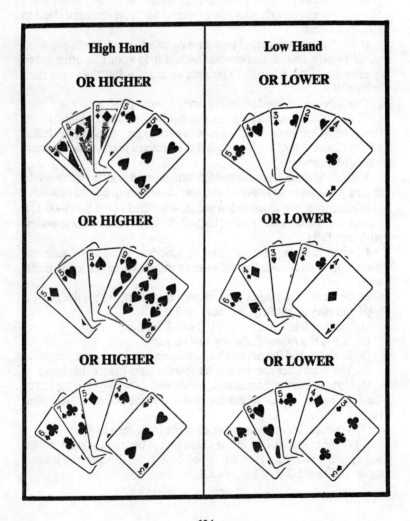

High Hand	Low Hand
OR HIGHER	**OR LOWER**
OR HIGHER	**OR LOWER**
OR HIGHER	**OR LOWER**

This method for beating lowball is *extremely* simple, but you'll find it effective and profitable.

Count the number of players remaining to your *left* up to and including the blind.

If the number is...
4, 5, 6, or 7, it's *Condition Sad;*
2 or 3, it's *Condition Happy;*
1, it's *Condition Attack;*
0, it's *Condition Blind* (your count will be 0 only if you *are* the blind).

Note: Most poker books speak of player positions beginning with #1 (immediately to the dealer's left) and increasing clockwise so that, in an eight-handed game, the dealer's position is #8. As far as I know, Norman Zadeh in *Winning Poker Systems* was the first to use the excellent method of counting the players remaining to act.

Important: When you're the first player (besides the blind) to enter a pot, this strategy dictates that you *always raise,* never just call. (See Figure 18-1.)

Although followers of my more advanced writing may quibble with the simplicity of this formula, it *does* win easily against the kind of unsophisticated competition you find in public card parlors.

It is customary for the first player in the pot to *raise.* Occasionally, an opponent just *calls,* and this can cause problems. My smoothed-out advice is: If your opponent has called (rather than raised) the blind, *never* raise. If you have a playing hand, merely call.

Your crash course makes it easy to decide what to do when someone has already raised. No matter what your *Condition,* re-raise with a pat seven or better or a one-card draw to a six-high or better. Otherwise, pretend that your opponent is following the chart you've just seen and *call* if your hand is at least as good as what he would have needed to raise.

In other words, if he raises from *Condition Sad,* then no matter what your *Condition* is, you need a hand equal to what *you* would have raised with had you been in his position. If your hand is weaker than what *his* requirement should be, *pass.*

There is one critical exception to this calling criteria: *Never call with a two-card draw.* If you're an experienced player, you've noticed that my two-card-draw raising advice is fairly liberal. But that's if you're the *first* player to charge *only!*

What to Raise With Before the Draw
If Everyone Before you Has Passed:

Condition	Pat Hand	1-Card Draw	2-Card Draw
Sad (no joker)	9-7-6-5-4	7-5-4-3	none
Sad (with joker)	9-8-7-6-joker	7-6-5-joker	none
Happy (no joker)	9-8-7-6-5	8-7-6-5	5-4-3
Happy (w/joker)	9-8-7-6-joker	8-7-6-joker	7-6-joker
Attack (no joker)	10-9-8-7-6	10-8-7-6	7-6-5
Attack (w/joker)	J-10-9-8-joker	10-9-8-joker	8-7-joker

Figure 18-1

If you've read any of the earlier crash courses, you know that I'm not going to provide advice on *all* situations, only *key* situations. In all other instances, my assumption is that you'll use your own best judgment and that it will be fairly average.

The last major category of advice is what to do when you're the blind.

I suppose some of you lowball sophisticates are annoyed because this strategy doesn't flow uniformly and fit nicely on bell curves. For instance, if an opponent raises in *Condition Happy,* how come the minimum pat calling hand for the blind is a straight nine *with or without* the joker? Doesn't the joker make a difference?

Yes, as I've pointed out in the past, the joker makes a great deal of difference! Still, here's a formula that works just the way it is! It's *my* recipe, so don't mess with the ingredients or I won't be responsible for the way it tastes.

Lastly, let's look at a few other essentials. After the draw, if you and an opponent have both drawn one or more cards, bet any ten or better, *always*. (The previous statement applies whether you're first to act or have already been checked into. By the way, the conventional rule in California is that you *must* bet a seven or better after the draw.)

Bluff after the draw with any pair of fours or higher.

Never enter a pot with the intention of bluffing. *There is no situation in lowball where you would show a profit barging into the pot with a hand like* 4-4-4-8-8. (If you can't trust your Poker Buddy, who can you trust?)

137

If you have a pat nine or ten with a one-card seven draw (or better), it's usually best *not to stand pat*. In fact, for the purpose of simplicity, I'm instructing you to stand pat *only* if you're against a *single* opponent who has already drawn at least two cards.

You should usually draw one card to this hand:

Most money is lost at lowball because players become emotionally upset. There's a great deal of short-term luck involved, and you'll need to develop a stable temperament. Without it, you're apt to find your mind short-circuited after a few bad beats. Your fingers will begin to fling chips toward the center of the table without your permission. This is known in the industry as "lowball reflex."

You might find it difficult to leave the table, especially when you're losing. In fact, you could even wither away and die. So please be careful.

PART EIGHT

The Magic of Probability

"In the beginning, everything
was even money."

Chapter 19

The War Against Probability

During the flight from Los Angeles to Vegas, I'd tried to convince my buddy not to play roulette. I stressed that blackjack would be much better, since he knew basic strategy.

His argument went like this: "All I gotta do is bet black. I don't say it works for everyone, but I've beat the hell out of the Sahara six trips in a row! Black just seems to keep running for me."

Using my very best debating techniques, I laid the Law of Averages on him. Finally, he seemed to grasp the concept that, although luck might save him for a while, sooner or later he had to go busted at the roulette wheel.

When we arrived at the Sahara, I headed for the poker room and my friend went off in quest of his blackjack fortune. A couple of hours later, he approached my poker table with winnings of $2800.

"Isn't that better than roulette?" I asked smugly.

His eyes sparkled mischievously, "It *was* roulette, Mike. I went up to the wheel and I remembered what you said about the Law of Averages. But I didn't see anyone big enough to enforce it!"

This chapter will be a disappointment to anyone who looks to the Law of Averages for salvation. You'll learn that things don't always break even as quickly as you might suspect.

No one can promise that if you flip a coin all day long, half the time you'll get heads. I can project, but I cannot promise.

A lot of people think the Law of Averages ensures that things will pretty much even out over a lifetime. That definitely isn't the case. You merely have to look around you and see that some humans, beginning with similar ability and opportunity, have prospered due to good fortune while others have failed, fallen sick or lived in pain.

So immediately we can discard the notion that life will necessarily be "fair" to us. But what about gambling? You find books on poker explaining that over the course of a year, a player will make about what he should. Who writes that junk?

Let's say you play five days a week, every week for a year, six hours per session. That's 1560 hours. Enough hands will have been played after that length of time for the result to be a fair representation of your abilities. Right?

No, that's wrong! Eloise Newell — who also happens to be a superb poker player — logged 20 days of $20-limit draw poker in January and broke exactly even. For the sake of convenience, I'm using those 20 days to illustrate a point.

These were Eloise's day-by-day results:

Date	$ Result
4	+420
6	+780
7	-285
8	+1500
9	-330
10	-1150
11	+285
12	-95
16	+805
17	-180
18	-1800
22	+1165
23	+400
24	+335
25	-600
26	-255
27	-1245
28	+295
29	+560
30	-605

The way I normally run a computer simulation, using results such as these, is to take the average daily result (in this case 0) in conjunction with a statistical figure called the standard deviation. Then I use those figures to generate hypothetical results at random.

For simplicity, I've devised another method that will be easier for the reader to understand. You have seen a list of actual results chosen because the total is even. Let's suppose that these results represent a true indication of a player's prospects. How can we project a hypothetical year? This method would be fair:

We'll put each of the 20 daily outcomes on a sheet of paper, fold and shuffle them in a hat. We'll draw one out at random and that will represent the first-day result. Then we'll refold that paper and place it back in the hat. Stir the papers around. Pick the second-day result.

Got it? You can see that this is perfectly fair, although it doesn't allow for results other than the ones actually produced in the 20-day test period. (Using the *mean* together with the *standard deviation,* we could have projected a win like $203, which was not on the list. We are NOT using the normal statistical method; we are proving a point.)

The computer faithfully accomplished what I ordered it to do. Using Eloise's January results, it projected 1000 years of poker. You can think of these results as indicating either of two things:

(1) They are the hypothetical future for one break-even player for the next 1000 years;

(2) They are a simulation of the fates of 1000 break-even players for the next year.

Either way, each computer year impartially represents 1560 hours of play. The 1000-year experiment registered an average (mean profit of $204.30. That implies that the computer ran "lucky" by $204,000 for 1,560,000 simulated hours. That's 13 cents an hour — not as surprising as it may seem to the typical Law-of-Averages worshipper.

Remember: In order to make this projection understandable to the reader, I restricted the program to randomly generating results exactly as they appeared on the 20-day list. The inability to smooth out the results by using mean and standard deviation causes short-term results to be slightly more erratic. The yearly projections, however, are very close to what they would be if a more precise method were used.

(Also keep in mind that this search is based on a highly volatile game — $20 limit with a $5 ante. The $20 applies to the bet *before* the draw; it's $40 *after.* When no one opens, more antes are added, and the limits are raised until the game becomes $50 before the draw and $100 after with $20 per player ante. Naturally, year-to-year results will be more erratic than with conservatively structured games.)

Ready for this? Best year: Win $36,810. Worst year: Lose $42,360.

Hey! Don't just breeze by those numbers. Go back and look again. Whereas the $79,170 difference between the best and worst performance would be a fluke, differences of $40,000 to $50,000 from year to year were very common!

What's the message? Suppose two guys come to Gardena (where poker is legal) at the same time. Neither is a super player. In fact, we know they both should only break even in the long run. If player A won $25,000 in the first year and player B lost $25,000, what do you think would happen?

Player B would go to player A and beg for lessons, right? The blind leading the blind! More than that, there was one winning streak of nine years that totaled more than $150,000, and an eight-year drought that cost $120,000. Can you imagine the player who suffered this loss trying to convince the other that there was no difference between their skills?

Does this mean, in view of such mammoth fluctuations in fate, that it doesn't pay to play solid poker?

Of course it pays. Based on this study, a player who was $30 an hour better than break-even would probably never have a losing year in 1000. He'd still have vast fluctuations, but these would only affect the *amount won*.

If you've been guilty of putting too much short-term importance on the Law of Averages, let me shake your faith a little further. My computer experiments have shown that 1000 baseball players whose true batting average was .295 ranged in season performance from under .200 to .407 at bat.

One player will be shipped to the minor leagues, never to return, while another becomes a national hero! And it's pure dumb luck!

For you probability purists, I'll point out that in real life .295 hitters don't go to the plate with the same expectation every time. This represents a slight flaw in the computer program, which always generated a random 29.5% chance of getting a hit.

The simplification *does* increase the fluctuations somewhat. If, as tends to be the actual fact, the batter sometimes has a 35% chance of getting a hit and sometimes 24%, he'd still expect a .295 average in the long run, but with smaller year-by-year fluctuations.

This hard-to-grasp concept can be demonstrated by imagining an extreme situation. Suppose a little-league batter has a .500 average against a pitcher. If this average were a true representation of his ability, then in four times at bat he might go 4-for-4, 0-for-4 or anything between.

If the experiment is repeated game after game, he'll have large fluctuations in his day-to-day batting, although his long-range expectation is still .500.

But what if, instead, our .500 batter faces a perfect pitcher the first two times at bat. This pitcher will *always* strike him out. Later in each game he'll bat twice against a terrible pitcher who will *always* surrender a home run. The little bastard will average .500 without *any* fluctuation if this experiment is repeated day after day.

This extreme example *never* happens in real life. The plain honest-to-Mike truth is that there's a whole world of gamblers out there. Some of them aren't getting their fair share of luck, and some never will!

So don't be discouraged. Whatever your game, get the biggest edge possible. That way you'll probably prosper quickly.

What if, alas, you must deal with tiny advantages? If you expect to win in the long run, stop thinking mile and imagine the Boston Marathon!

Chapter 20

"Experts" Who Destroy Your Bankroll

When I was nine years old, Dad put a tent in our back yard. It was a present, a special place for my friends and me. It became sacred ground, a clubhouse where no adult dared enter lest he encounter our scorn.

Every time you stepped inside, you would be enveloped by the smell of canvas. It was a very old tent, patched in spots that hinted of nameless accidents in the woods.

Just follow along for a minute. We'll be getting to the point.

A Coleman lantern hung inside — you know, the kind where you can adjust the light anywhere from bright down to eerie. The brighter it burned, the more you'd smell the kerosene.

Sometimes, when the weather was good, Mom would let me sleep out there with three or four friends. I'd turn the Coleman so low that it almost went out. Then I'd give it a soft shove and it would swing back and forth from it's handle. Spooky, sinister shadows would twist across the army cots and the sleeping bags. At times the wind would conveniently lean against the walls of the tent, cooperating with the creepy mood we all wished upon ourselves.

The point? Yeah, well, we're getting closer.

Of course, we weren't really frightened. Not terribly. We had to work at it just to get those tiny shivers to sneak up and down our spines. So we'd tell ghost stories.

There was this kid, Edward. For some reason, nobody ever called him Ed. He was the best ghost storyteller among us, and he'd paint haunting word pictures for hours. Sometimes he'd whisper solemnly, creating true ghosts and real victims.

You could tell that he believed these things himself.

Whenever the lantern swung too slowly, one of us would give it another push. Then there were unshapely shadows to terrify us as they danced and became tangled.

"We can never tell anyone," said Edward. "We all have to

promise."

So we promised not to tell our parents, because they might laugh and offer some stupid adult logic. Such rebuttal would be most unwelcome to us; besides, no one really wanted to share our experiences with skeptics.

So we pledged our silence, all of us, and we maintained it.

I heard from Edward the other day. His letter said that he's been going to Vegas twice each year.

He explained that he'd been following my columns and had been meaning to get in touch. "I have stumbled on something I bet you might find interesting. Certain numbers keep turning up at keno all the time, particularly when they follow certain other numbers that can be figured quite simply, but no one knows about this. That is not even the most amazing part. What really seems exciting to me and my wife is the unbelievable fact that the same thing happens when we use our system for roulette. Namely, we win!"

Should he send me the details?

No! Don't send them! I'm tired of reading about using psychic weapons against roulette wheels and charting numbers at craps. I used to laugh about attacking slot machines astrologically and beating keno by analyzing mysterious number sequences. But when you consider that people are following this advice and destroying their bankrolls, it seems serious.

It's not just which numbers you bet, they tell me. It's also *when* you bet and *how much* you bet.

Poor souls! They must lie around all day determining what comes next in a betting sequence like 3-5-2-1-7. Such analysis takes a great deal of time. Do you suppose these guys ever get laid?

If you sprinkle in a few relevant facts, like the date of your birth, you can begin to appreciate the numerology of gambling. There ought to be a lot of winning systems that grow out of this sort of dedicated investigation.

But, alas, there aren't any. And there never will be, because it's all bullshit! Well, maybe that's a little strong. Let me think for a minute and see if I can rephrase that...

Nope, can't. It's bullshit, and the more I think about it, the angrier I get. You see, there are some of us who've put a lot of effort into supplying the serious gambler with real, meaningful answers. To do this requires logic, disciplined evaluation and a certain degree of insight. The science of gambling is often complex, and scarcely anyone understands it thoroughly.

Many people are too busy with their own problems and professions to learn the tough, entangled world of scientific wagering. That's understandable. I don't have the time or the inclination to unravel the complexities of modern medicine. For that, I respect the advice of my doctor. When confronted by a legal dilemma, I seek a lawyer.

Serious gamblers deserve the advice of legitimate gaming authorities. *Gambling Times Magazine* provides the opportunity to find that advice. But the newsstands are peppered with gambling garbage — systems that tell you how much to bet, how to manage your roulette money, or magic ways to win at keno.

By the way, I haven't forgotten about the tent in the back yard. . . or Edward. . . or the point.

This is a chart that lists some common things you can gamble on: each has an accompanying word that lets you know, once and for all, whether that game can be beaten.

Name of the Game	Is Winning Possible?
Baccarat	Possibly
Backgammon	Yes
Baseball betting	Yes
Bingo	No
Blackjack	Yes
Boxing betting	Yes
Bridge	Yes
Chuck-a-Luck	No
Craps	No
Dog Race betting	Yes
Faro	No
Football betting	Yes
Gin Rummy	Yes
Harness Racing	Yes
Hockey betting	Yes
Horse Race betting (thoroughbred)	Yes
Jai Alai	Yes
Keno	No

Keno machines	No
Liars' Poker	Yes
Lotteries	No
Money Wheel	No
Numbers Games	No
Over and Unders (Sports bet)	Yes
Poker	Yes
Poker Machines (Video, progressive)	Yes
Pyramid Games	Yes
Roulette	No
Slot Machines, non-progressive	No
Slot Machines, progressive	Yes

Of course, the list could include hundreds of other things. I have omitted most card games. Had they been included, all but a few would have been given a "yes." That's because most card games pit opponent against opponent and the more skillful players prosper.

You can invent special propositions. You can bet whether a flea will die on its flight over the Antarctic. There are, in truth, limitless ways to win at gambling. With all this potential for a dedicated gambler, you wonder why writers spend so much time devising "magic" systems to do the impossible.

Let's talk about the chart. Of the 30 things listed, 17 were theoretically beatable, 12 were not and there was a "possibly." That latter was given to Baccarat.

Pyramid games? Maybe you're surprised by the "yes." These games received a lot of publicity about a year ago, especially in California. I won't take time to explain how they work, but basically a person willingly hands over some money to someone else. This is the buy-in. He then solicits others to give *him* money and join the game. The amount of money you get is determined by your position on a "pyramid." This scam, like pyramid letters, is illegal. So why did I include it on the chart? To correct a common misconception.

Many newspapers quoted mathematics professors who asserted that since each newcomer to the game had to recruit two others, the supply of investors would soon be exhausted. Well, that's certainly true. But the implication was that you couldn't beat the pyramid game. And that's certainly false.

The common sense of this is that the first players in the game couldn't possibly lose, and the last players — when a pyramid collapsed — couldn't possibly win. All the money lost was won by others. The net was zero. Obviously the advantage went to early arrivals and to those skilled in convincing others to join.

I don't want you to look at the chart and get the idea that everything marked "yes" is easy to beat. In fact, some of these things are very hard to conquer without special knowledge and training.

Here are some absolute truths . . .

(1) You must eventually lose if the odds are against you;

(2) You must eventually win if the odds are in your favor;

(3) If the odds are flexible and dependent on how you play, you can favorably affect the outcome by using skill. This does not always mean that you can win — only that if you play skillfully, you will improve your chances;

(4) If skill affects the odds in any way, then skillful players will eventually fare better than unskillful players.

Now here's another absolute truth. This is the one that all those magic-system writers seem to ignore: *If the odds are against you, it doesn't matter how you vary the amounts of your bets, you will eventually lose.*

That means you'd be wasting your time trying to devise methods of betting for games where the odds are fixed against you. Games such as roulette, keno and craps offer no opportunity to win in the long run. That's why there are professional blackjack players, professional poker players and professional football handicappers while, in the whole damn world, there's not one single professional craps shooter.

So, if you play craps, do it for the excitement and try to defy the odds for a while. A lot of people find it worth the price. Remember, some craps bets are better than others, but none is profitable.

And here's a bonus absolute truth: *If the odds are against you, it doesn't matter which numbers or colors you choose, you will eventually lose.*

Let's get back to the original point. Reading Edward's letter, it occurred to me that he had never escaped the tent in my back yard. He was still finding mysterious truths that bore no logic but sent shivers up and down his spine.

A lantern still swung in his mind, and strange shadows danced on the walls. For him it wasn't ghosts anymore. It was gambling. Thinking back, I could still feel the uncertain excitement of those nights in my tent.

The point? It's there. And when you see it, you'll understand why some people spend their whole lives questing for the perfect keno system.

Beware, my friends, because scientists can only search and charlatans will always see.

Chapter 21

Safe and Sane Probability

"You like probability, don't you?" Uncle Jake quizzed. His tone was accusing and his short grey whiskers seemed to bristle (which is one of the things whiskers do best). Now he glared at me with eyes that simultaneously seemed tired and sparkling.

This was 1967, maybe 1968, in Grass Valley, California — a town 100 miles or so northeast of San Francisco. But let's get things straight right away. This was not *my* Uncle Jake; this was *everybody's* Uncle Jake.

The clerk at the country store (where I was buying a sufficient supply of candy bars to last the next 100 miles of mountain highway to Lake Tahoe) addressed him as Uncle Jake. Then two small boys, ages four and seven from left to right, called him Uncle Jake and bought bubble gum. Next, some snippy 75-year-old woman strode in and snapped, "Get out of my way, Uncle Jake!" She breezed by him with scarcely a glance, then ordered the clerk to, "Get me a pack of them Camels, no filters."

"I asked if you like probability," Uncle Jake reminded, ignoring the woman who spun around to glare spitefully.

She said, "Don't go botherin' the young man about all that arithmetic bullshit. He don't wanna hear it and nobody else in Grass Valley wants to hear it. You come here all educated and try to make friends with us folk. Well, some of us lived hereabouts fifty years and we don't need no one comin' around with your science of probables and not probables, showin' us how to run our businesses. Hell, you're scarin' off half the customers in town. You look like a bum! And you say you was a college professor. Just look at you, Mr. Mathematician! You're a joke! Ha!" She stormed to the exit.

"And one more thing — you ain't nobody's uncle, so from now on I'll just call you Jake like you was a normal human being, even though you ain't." Then she left.

"Let me tell you about probabilities," Uncle Jake persisted, oblivious to our rude interruption. "I taught the *science* of probability at Cornell. This was back before WWII. Nobody knew a thing about it. Nobody does today, either. Want a little lesson? Okay, what's you're name, anyway?"

"Mike."

"Okay, Mike, would you agree that birds don't understand probability?"

This was 15 years ago, and I was heavy into debating and not very keen on diplomacy. So here stood some ancient gadfly pestering me about something for which I had a pretty good feel — probability. That's why I decided to surprise him. "Sure, I think birds understand probability. When you approach them, they get scared and fly off. But first they wait to see how close you'll come. At some point they figure that their present comfort is outweighed by the *probability* of danger. That's when they fly away."

Feeling smug about the precision of my words, I finally lifted my face and sought his eyes. I found them friendly. He said, "You make a good case, son, so I won't flunk you."

Unexpectedly, he took several steps toward the door, then paused before leaving. I never saw that face again; his back was to me as he spoke. From somewhere within me radiated an unnatural chill that tickled from the base of my spine to my neck. It was as if I sensed the presence of a North American guru; and I knew his next words would be important.

"But you're wrong, Mike. If birds understood probability, they wouldn't grow feathers." As he passed through the door without turning, he raised his hand and briskly waved good-bye.

"That there is one crazy lunatic," laughed the clerk.

Maybe the clerk was right. You see, I never did figure Uncle Jake out. Were his last words just a jest or had he intended some revelation? I thought about it on the road to Tahoe. Finally I decided there was a 60% chance the man was crazy, a 25% chance he had uttered some truth that eluded me and a 15% chance there was some miscellaneous explanation. Chalking percentages on my mental blackboard is a habit I've carried with me since high school. While the most common use is for poker, sports and spur-of-the-moment wagers, I try to predict people's behavior, too.

It's important that you believe that the previous Grass Valley episode was not contrived. It happened exactly that way, and it stands today as one of my most peculiar experiences. If Uncle Jake had cornered me about botany, it would have been a less memorable day. Arguments about probability are rare in rural America.

At the risk of being obscure (and confusing you the same way that Uncle Jake confused me), I've decided to explain probability in my own fashion. Many gamblers hate the word, preferring to substitute terms such as *chance, price, odds* and *line.*

All right, it's healthy to hold a grudge against subjects that are taught merely as mental disciplines. That's why, for many, *Latin* is lousy and *fractions* aren't friendly. Frequently, you must understand what a subject *is* before you can profit from it. They tell you probability is about *bell curves, Bernoulli trials* and *binomial distribution.* They preach *doubly stochastic matrices* and *discrete sample space.* There's really nothing wrong with that, if it makes them feel good. But probability is the most important force governing our lives — every day, all the time. And it ought to be given a bit more respect. It is both fragile and overpowering; and it is fundamentally religious.

What comes next is more philosophical than practical. The practical will come later when we begin to explore easy ways to figure the odds. Right now, let's examine the truth about probability.

Caro's First (and only) Great Law of Probability: *In the beginning everything was even-money.*

Yeah, I know, that sounds a little like, "If birds understood probability, they wouldn't grow feathers." But what we're dealing with here is the supreme truth that governs how frequently you get blackjack and how often the dice roll over on seven. We're talking about pure, primitive, essential *power.* The power that makes the Dolphins a 2-point pick over the Jets, the power that makes it worth trying to draw a flush if you're getting 10 to one on your money.

Before the AFL merged with the NFL, even before there was professional football, back when nobody played poker, there was only a universal emptiness.

Some say there was just a vacuum of starless, atomless space. But vacuum is a bad word because, it seems to me, vacuum must relate in some way to something nearby which is *not* a vacuum. We're talking way back before the very first gods, before there were any governing forces, before there was any conscious thought. Not even one lonely amoeba swam the great oceans of earth. We're talking long before there even *was* earth. We're talking hundreds of years ago, baby!

Now, suppose you could be transported back to the moment when reality rooted. Say you had some conscious faculties but had no knowledge of events that happened beyond the origin.

You feel empty, apart from yourself. You are not truly alive because you have no surroundings. Suddenly you're tipped off that a universe is about to appear. "Oh, wow, a universe!" you think. You get really excited. Your heart starts racing like crazy. Let's ignore the Big Bang Theory, because that's messy. Our coming universe will be either black sprinkled with white stars or white sprinkled with black stars.

So, go ahead and make the line. Since you don't have any information, you can't reason that black is a more traditional background for sky. You can't suppose that white would make the stars show up better or that hot things are seldom black. You don't even know what hot is. Way, way beyond your comprehension is stuff like: White is the presence of all color and black is the absence of all color. You don't know anything.

So, you'd better make the line even-money and hope nobody has better information than you do.

A similar example — suppose I say, "Hey, there are two football teams about to kick off at the playground down the street. I'll call them Team Y and Team Z. Make a line and I'll give you a bet."

You wouldn't blurt, "Okay, I make Team Z a 14-point favorite." If you were daring enough to venture a line, it would be even-money.

Maybe all this seems trivial, but it isn't. Here's the point: Probability deals with *uncertainty*. Shuffle a deck and pick a card. It's even money that it will be red, right? True, but what are we measuring? How much we know about a deck of cards? No, how much we *don't* know about the outcome.

If you had perfect information, you'd be able to measure the mental state of the shuffler and chart his strength, his adrenaline flow and all distractions which could influence him. You could compute his dexterity and calculate the changing positions of the cards during the shuffle. Finally, taking these and trillions of other factors into consideration, you could know *for certain* whether the top card would be red or black. But human intelligence is far too meager to master most of this, so we're relegated to believing that outcomes are uncertain, even though they are absolute.

Some mathematicians may argue that I'm missing the point. Probability was developed on the assumption that results are random and formulas were created with randomness in mind. But in the whole history of the universe there has never been a random event. Everything happens because of everything else that has already happened. The result of a coin flip *appears* random to us because we are not sophisticated enough to calculate the outcome. Too many variables. A severely retarded child might view punishment as a purely random tragedy, having no correlation with behavior. You and I are smarter, so it takes more to confuse us.

Mostly we gamblers use probability to estimate the chances based on the little we know relative to a great group of things which we assume *nobody* knows.

The first thing you must learn is that probability is not poison. It's the most powerful force in the universe because it is *every* force in the universe. It governs your fate, gives you birth and makes you die. It causes your team to fumble on the goal line and sometimes fattens your wallet. You can either fear it or make friends with it — that's up to you.

Now that you have my First Great Law of Probability, I'll leave you with my definition: *Probability is a measure of ignorance.* No more, no less.

Ask any penguin. Penguins are flightless birds — and you seldom see their feathers.

Chapter 22

Fun With Probability Strips

How does probability work? Maybe that's a good question and maybe it isn't. If I were inclined to dabble in semantics, I would point out that probability doesn't work; probability predicts. But I am not so inclined and anyway, today is Tuesday. (Try guessing the odds against me saying that.)

The last chapter was flagrantly philosophic. You learned Caro's First Great Law of Probability; *In the beginning everything was even-money.* That means, in the absence of information, every bet should be straight-up.

Now we're going to be less obscure and more practical. Some of you will find this introduction to probability too elementary. Maybe you should read it anyway and maybe you shouldn't.

You can't learn probability by sitting in the shade and waiting for it to reveal itself. Even standing in the sun would mean a very long wait. What's worse, you'll never learn probability from some mathematics teacher who has simply swallowed formulas. Unfortunately, learning probability takes a little effort; it requires rolling up your sleeves, bracing yourself and cutting some paper.

So, get out your scissors. Find yourself a sheet of paper. Do it now; I'm not fooling around! I'll assume that your page is about 8½" by 11" (which is standard typewriter size), but almost any size will do, so long as the shape is rectangular.

Now snip this sucker into 10 strips. Each strip should be about the same width as any other, but there's no problem if you mess up a bit. Also, it doesn't matter whether you decide to cut horizontally or vertically. If your strips are all the same length, that's plenty to please me.

Above: Your Paper
Before Probability Incisions

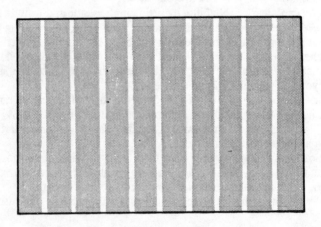

Above: 10 Strips of Paper After Incisions

Suppose two evenly matched football teams decide to play two games. Just to get you involved, we'll say that one team (yours) is fighting for universal bliss while the second team (your enemy) is intending to shut down half the poker rooms in America. Unfortunately, the agreement stipulates that your team must win *both* games to achieve universal bliss. As you can see, the stakes are pretty high here.

What are the chances that your team will win both games, assuming a tie is impossible? While this answer is known instantly by many gamblers, some of those have trouble understanding the reason. Others wrongly assume that it's 2 to 1, which has a good sound to it.

You're probably wondering what to do with all those strips of paper, right? Have you ruined a piece of paper for nothing? Maybe you have and maybe you haven't.

The first thing to do is stop saying "strips of paper." You must give them more credibility. What you have created are 10 *probability strips,* so treat them with respect.

A few teachers, especially those with statistical backgrounds, proudly explain probability in terms of pies. They draw perfect circles and cut the proportions into wedge-shaped slices. Why wear out your scissors creating fancy wedges when you could simply snip off portions of a probability strip?

In order to reason out the odds against your team winning both games, let's pick up one probability strip and examine it. Look at this strip closely. It represents the *entire* spectrum of outcomes for the two games. It is 100% of what our chance of success (i.e., winning both games) would be if nothing could prevent it.

Get your scissors ready for some really serious calculating.

Since our team and our opponent are evenly matched, then we must assume that, on the first game, we're entitled to half the strip of paper. If we tried this proposition over and over again forever, half the time we'll still be eligible for universal bliss after the first game; half the time we will have already failed and poker rooms will be closing all over the place.

Reason along with me. In order to win *both* games, our team must win the *first* game. If we lose this initial contest, then nothing else matters; we *failed to satisfy the condition* that both games be won.

Here's where you get to make your first cut. You see, much of probability can be calculated by evaluating the various sequences of minor outcomes that make up the whole event. In this case, the whole event is the outcome of both games, but we've defined success as winning twice. Remember, we're only interested in finding the odds against that success. Nothing else matters.

Remember, our original probability strip represents 100% success. How much of this success should we lose after the first game? If we could see the future, then we'd either lose all of the strip (if our team lost) or none of it (if our team won), but we can't. The only thing to do is to apportion the strip fairly. How much of this 100% success will our opponents deny us after the first game? Snip it off. Don't be afraid — you've got more probability strips than you'll need. (By the way, this experiment will work more smoothly if you cut across the width, rather than making a lengthwise separation.)

If you did it right, you cut your strip *in half*. That's because our opponents were just as likely to win the first game as we were. Now pick up the piece of strip you just sliced away and make it *"Opponent Wins First Game — Proposition Fails."* While still holding what remains of the original strip in your hand (the half that measures your success), mark it *"My Team Wins First Game — Proposition Still Alive."*

Place the piece you've cut away neatly on the table; you'll be using it shortly. Now let's examine the second game. For the sake of this discussion, we'll assume that the outcome of the first game did not change the odds. Both teams are still evenly matched and it's even-money that we'll win the second game. You are holding the *remaining* chance of success. Considering what *remains* of your probability strip only, cut it fairly into your team's share for winning the second game and your opponent's share.

Done? Well, again you should have halved the strip you're holding. Another piece has fallen away and what remains tight between your fingers is your chance of winning the two-game proposition. Now mark the piece that's just fallen away *"Opponent Wins Second Game After Losing First — Proposition Fails."* Next, mark the piece left in your hand *"My Team Wins Both Games — Universal Bliss."*

Now place all the pieces of your original probability strip on the table. Using a piece of tape, attach the pieces that contain the word *"Fails."* How does this restructured strip of failure compare with the last remaining piece in your hand? It's about three times as large, isn't it? And guess what? The odds against your team successfully winning both games are exactly 3 to 1. It looks bad for poker.

Mathematically, you can reassure yourself by saying there are two possible outcomes for the first game (win or lose) and two possible outcomes for the second game, so there are a total of 2 × 2 possible outcomes of the two-game event. That's four outcomes and only one of those — win-win — will bring success. Therefore the odds against success are 3 to 1. More precisely, without using numbers at all, the chance against success is lose-lose and lose-win and win-lose & (failure) vs. win-win.

Some of you familiar with elementary probability might be used to obtaining the same answer by multiplying .5 × .5 and getting .25, which translates to 25% success, leaving 75% for failure. The correlation between odds, fractions and percentage is very simple, but I'll leave that for some future discussion.

Right now, I want you to think in terms of probability strips. The importance of these strips of paper goes way beyond measuring the chances of winning two games in a row. You'd be surprised at what you can do with these little darlings.

Suppose you wish to calculate the odds against the Los Angeles Dodgers sweeping a three-game series from the Atlanta Braves. Sports fans frequently choose to make bets like this, although the lines they come up with are sometimes outrageous. The first thing you should do is examine the games one by one, using the starting pitchers to give you an idea of what the lines will be on each game.

Say the Dodgers are favored by 2 to 1 to win the first game. The second game looks like even-money and the Dodgers are a 3 to 2 favorite in the third contest. Use one of your spare probability strips and see if you can approximate the right odds. I'll wait.

Okay. Here's how you should have done it:

Looking at the first game, you should have cut away one-third of your strip. That's because if this game were played a million times, the Braves would win about one-third of the games. Any time the Braves win, the Dodgers can't sweep the series, so the proposition fails one-third of the time on the very first game. Now your strip is only two-thirds its original size.

The second game is even-money, so what's left of your probability strip must be cut in half, letting the piece that represents a Braves win fall away. What remains is the probability that the Dodgers will win the first two games.

What about the third game? That 3 to 2 really means this: Out of five games (3 + 2), the Dodgers could be expected to win three, the Braves two. If the Braves win, that spells failure for our proposition. So 2/5

(40%) of our remaining probability strip gets cut away, because it belongs to the Braves and means curtains for the Dodgers' sweep.

Now put all the pieces you've cut away back together and match them against the remaining strip in your hand. How many times as large is the combined portion of discarded paper compared to the surviving strip? Well, those are your odds against the Dodgers taking all three games of the series.

Mathematically, you simply multiply your probability of winning one game by the probability of winning the next. This is your chance of staying alive; the rest gets cut away mathematically (instead of going through the physical effort of cutting paper). So: .667 (a two-thirds chance of winning the first game) × .5 (even-money on the second) × .6 (three-fifths on the final game). The answer is 20% success (.2), just as if we had used a probability strip. The 80% failure (which you clipped away) was four times as large as your 20% success. The correct odds against the sweep were four to one. Was the remaining strip in your hand about one-fourth as large as all the paper you cut away?

Naturally, there are more sophisticated techniques to learn, and these probability strips aren't practical when the odds are very long. (It's hard to estimate the difference between 500 to 1 and 750 to 1 with strips of paper.) The important thing is that you now understand where probability lives. It is neither mind-boggling nor mysterious.

The probability of anything being successful is always, conceptually, a whole strip of paper minus the amount cut away by the chance of failure. It can never be greater or less than the size of the paper you began with. That's why mathematicians are fond of saying that the probability of something always falls between zero and one.

I could go on, but I'm finished.

PART NINE

Dessert—An Extra Chapter

"It demonstrates how
thoroughly people can be
enveloped in a net of their own
design."

Chapter 23

Bye-Bye Crazyman

This was supposed to be a truly important chapter about mathematical mistakes made in professional sports. I could've shown why you should be reluctant to bet teams which, although they may seem statistically superior, repeatedly make the same strategic errors.

You would have learned that these errors were not so much mistakes of a high mathematical order, but rather they were — most of the time — breaches of logic.

Some of the more common of these:

(1) Professional football teams in evenly matched contests who, late in the fourth quarter, kick field goals from within the one-yard line to tie the game and send it into overtime;

(2) National League Baseball teams who, in the later innings, fail to replace a poor-hitting pitcher for a pinch batter because the pitcher has tossed a good game;

(3) Football teams who punt in situations when the correct gamble is to go for a first down;

(4) Basketball coaches who habitually bench star players when they get in foul trouble, saving their talents for later in the game; and

(5) *Any* baseball manager who uses the bunt as more than an occasional weapon.

You should slant your bets toward coaches who make correct decisions.

In years past, Notre Dame was extremely successful in key football games. They were perceived by the public and by other coaches as an almost-reckless, gambling team. In truth, I believe a great share of their success should be attributed to the fact that their flamboyant style more nearly approached a correct game strategy than their more-conservative opponents. The "Luck of the Irish" is a tribute to the power of probability.

Listen, folks, this could've been a hell of a chapter! So what happened, Mike? Why didn't you write it?

Well, I just remembered an article by David Sklansky that appeared in the June issue (1981) of *Gambling Times*. He deals with one particular mathematical error and how it applies to all phases of gambling, and also to football. It explores much of the terrain I had intended to trod. It's a brilliantly conceived article by a man I hold in the highest regard. Read it. In fact read *all* of Sklansky's *Gambling Times* articles, since they will help you deal with many of the concepts discussed here in this excellent book.

The first thing I give my poker students is a nifty little speech that goes something like this: "When you sit in a poker game, you will be allowed 20 minutes to establish yourself as *the* force to be reckoned with. Anytime you fail to do this, I am instructing you to *quit*. When you enter a game, it is *yours,* and you must permit no one to challenge you for supremacy at your table.

"I'll show you several ways and several images you can use to gain psychological leverage against your opponents. Why is this important? When your opponents are either intimidated or confused by you — or both — much of their mental energy is wasted worrying about what *you* are going to do. This limits their capacity to make rational decisions about their own hands."

Okay, one of the things I use to gain table supremacy is the "crazy image." Sometimes when playing five-card draw, I'll call an opener with:

and stand pat. When the opener checks after the draw, I simply spread these cards face-up on the table, making no attempt to win the pot. Of course, I'm surrendering whatever it costs me to call the opener, but that's very, very cheap advertising. A few plays like this and your opponents are so confused and amused that they're apt to giggle while giving you their money.

Twice world champion Doyle "Texas Dolly" Brunson was so impressed by the power of this strategy that he asked me to contribute two chapters to his 600-page poker manual. That part was fine with me, but in the process he decided to name me "Crazy Mike." The photo used in that book was the same one that appeared in my column in *Gambling Times* until April. It was the picture of a Wild Man.

Doyle has since become a truly great friend, but it's time to bury this "crazy" stuff, because that's just one of many images I use in poker games. Besides it conflicts with the serious work on theory and probability I intend to keep publishing.

Nevertheless, before we put "Crazy Mike" to rest, I want to share something that happened in Denver seven years ago. Every gambler has a favorite story, and this is mine.

Roughly every two years I flew to Denver, my hometown, because I enjoyed the Rockies where I spent time exploring the forests. Usually I don't get completely away from poker, since old friends will often invite me to their home games, and I have a hard time rejecting these offers.

On that trip, there was a dollar-limit game at Timothy's house. Here was a guy I used to pal around with in high school when we were members of the debate team. He was now nearing thirty, still in law school, and had turned into a very opinionated sort, using elaborate gestures whenever he spoke.

I won $68 using a particularly crazy image which was accompanied by a big "advertising" budget. This was an especially accelerated version of the crazy game, performed for Tim's benefit.

It was part of an elaborate plot. You see, the last time we played (about two years previously), he took me aside afterwards and lectured me at length about getting some discipline into my game. He fancied himself as an amateur psychologist and felt that a few sessions with him would do me a world of good.

Futilely, I'd tried to convince him that my unusual poker plays were part of an act calculated to throw my opponents off-guard and win chips, but he couldn't assimilate it. Finally, I'd figured, "Why bother?" Timothy had been evolving backward intellectually: Cro-Magnon to Java and you expected him to be swinging by his tail any year now.

This time I'd come to Denver prepared for the confrontation. As he cashed in my chips he said, with a certain snide sarcasm, "That was just an act again, huh, Mike? I mean all those silly plays. Look, don't feel bad. Even I have trouble bringing discipline into my life sometimes."

I said, accepting $88, which was my original buy-in plus profit, "Yeah, just an act Timmy. I don't have any discipline problems. I've seen you get pretty upset about some stuff that wouldn't even bother me." I deliberately measured my words to goad him out of his aura of self-assuredness. Addressing the other six former buddies surrounding us, I chided, "This guy threw a temper tantrum on the tennis court one day like you wouldn't believe!"

He grew really flustered. "Well, at least I didn't go around afterwards claiming it was only an act!"

The time was now perfect. I leaned back against the poker table, narrowed my eyes and glared at him. Suddenly I was screaming, "Look, I'm tired of this bullshit! Why don't you just take your goddamn poker game and stuff it!"

I began to tighten my muscles and tremble slightly. My breathing became forced. I grabbed a nearby ashtray and spilled the contents onto the floor. "And you can stuff this goddamn ashtray, too!" I ranted, flinging the plastic disk into a sofa across the room. My maniacal frenzy was such that I kicked at the tile floor and babbled incomplete sentences.

Finally, I wheeled and stormed toward the door.

"Don't leave," he pleaded. "Let's talk about it."

Dramatically, I paused at the doorway, then slowly, sadly walked back to the gathering of stunned onlookers.

Almost quietly, almost kindly, Tim said, "You see, Mike, that wasn't an act was it?"

"Maybe it was an act," I responded rather belligerently.

"You're only kidding yourself. Why not be honest?"

Up until then I had held my head shyly downward. Now I glared at him, forcing a spark of anger to my eyes. "You got a hundred dollars to lose?" I challenged.

He shrugged. "What have you got in mind?"

Knowing how he prided himself on his oratorical skills, I made this proposition: We would wager $100 and see if one of us could convince our six friends of the validity of our contentions. We would each have two minutes to speak before them. He could argue that I suffered a breakdown of discipline. I could try to convince our "jury" that what they had witnessed was purely an act.

Going first, he strutted before us, enjoying the stage. He looked at me and began, "I don't even care about the hundred bucks, Mike. If I can just help you see the truth, that will be my reward. There's no great shame in acting emotionally. We all do it." He knew he had me whipped, and he was being generous. But it was the type of warped generosity little people use to fuel their own egos.

He made a pretty good case out of it, talking about those human feelings every man shared and how we're much better off if we admit our weaknesses. No one, said he, is a superman. He went way past his allotted two minutes, but what did I care? The more he talked, the higher he climbed. At one point, his eyes met mine and you could read how hard he was hoping to reach me.

When it was my turn I stood before the group and sighed as if plotting where to begin. I stalled, enjoying the building suspense.

Then, removing a sheet of typing paper from my shirt pocket, I said in an unnaturally subdued voice, "This is something I wrote the other day. Before I say anything else, I'd like you guys to read it."

It was neatly typed on both sides of the page, double-spaced. I passed it first to a friend on the far side of the room so that Timmy would be the last to read it.

It said this:

"Caro leans on poker table and glares. Without provocation, he begins shouting, 'Look, I'm tired of this bullshit! Why don't you just take your goddamn poker game and stuff it!' He breathes hard, trembles. Grabs nearest ashtray, empties on floor, rages, 'You can stuff this goddamn ashtray, too!' Heaves ashtray hysterically across room..."

As I said, that's my favorite gambling experience. My friends have heard that story so many times, they're probably sick of it. It was a ploy that worked perfectly. And it demonstrates how thoroughly people can be enveloped in a net of their own design.

This is the day I say good-bye to "Crazy Mike" because, me, well... I'm sane as a soda cracker, and I intend to stay that way 'til the day of the drizzle.

KEEPING YOUR GAMING
KNOWLEDGE CURRENT

"The Mad Genius," Mike Caro, writes a monthly column for *Gambling Times* magazine called *Caro On Gambling*. Now that you've read Mike's book, you'll want to keep abreast of the rapid and continuous changes and developments in the gaming field. The best way to do that is with a subscription to *Gambling Times* magazine.

Since February of 1977, readers of *Gambling Times* magazine have profited immensely. They have done so by using the information they have read each month. If that sounds like a simple solution to winning more and losing less, well it is! Readers look to *Gambling Times* for that very specific reason. And it delivers.

Gambling Times is totally dedicated to showing readers how to win more money in every form of legalized gambling. How much you're going to win depends on many factors, but it's going to be considerably more than the cost of a subscription.

WINNING AND MONEY

Winning, that's what *Gambling Times* is all about. And money, that's what *Gambling Times* is all about. Because winning and money go hand in hand.

Here's what the late Vince Lombardi, the famous football coach of the Green Bay Packers, had to say about winning:

> "It's not a sometime thing. Winning is a habit. There is no room for second place. There is only one place in my game and that is first place. I have finished second twice in my time at Green Bay and I don't ever want to finish second again. The objective is to win—fairly, squarely, decently, by the rules—but to win. To beat the other guy. Maybe that sounds hard or cruel. I don't think it is. It is and has always been an American zeal to be first in anything we do, and to win, and to win and to win."

Mr. Lombardi firmly believed that being a winner is "man's finest hour." *Gambling Times* believes it is too, while being a loser is depressing, ego-deflating, expensive and usually very lonely. "Everybody loves a winner" may be a cliche, but it's true. Winners command respect and are greatly admired. Winners are also very popular and have an abundance of friends. You may have seen a winner in a casino, with a bevy of girls surrounding him...or remember one who could get just about any girl he wanted.

Some of the greatest gamblers in the world also have strong views on what winning is all about. Here's what two of them have to say on the subject:

"To be a winner, a man has to feel good about himself and know he has some kind of advantage going in. I never made bets on even chances. Smart is better than lucky."— "Titanic" Thompson

"When it comes to winnin', I got me a one-track mind. You gotta want to win more than anything else. And you gotta have confidence. You can't pretend to have it. That's no good. You gotta have it. You gotta know. Guessers are losers. Gamblin's just as simple as that."—Johnny Moss

Gambling Times will bring you the knowledge you need to come home a winner and come home in the money. For it is knowledge, the kind of knowledge you'll get in its pages, that separates winners from losers. It's winning and money that *Gambling Times* offers you. *Gambling Times* will be your working manual to winning wealth.

The current distribution of this magazine is limited to selected newsstands in selected cities. Additionally, at newsstands where it is available, it's being snapped up, as soon as it's displayed, by gamblers who know a sure bet when they see one.

So if you're serious about winning, you're best off subscribing to *Gambling Times*. Then you can always count on its being there, conveniently delivered to your mailbox—and what's more, it will be there one to two weeks before it appears on the newsstands. You'll be among the first to receive the current issue as soon as it comes off the presses, and being first is the way to be a winner.

Having every monthly issue of *Gambling Times* will enable you to build an "Encyclopedia of Gambling," since the contents of this magazine are full of sound advice that will be as good in five or ten years as it is now.

As you can see, a subscription to *Gambling Times* is your best bet for a future of knowledgeable gambling. It's your ticket to *WINNING* and *MONEY.*

Take the time to read the following offer. As you can see, *Gambling Times* has gone all out to give you outstanding bonuses. You can join the knowledgeable players who have learned that *Gambling Times* helps them to win more money.

FOUR NEW WAYS TO GET 12 WINNING ISSUES OF *GAMBLING TIMES* FREE...

Every month over 250,000 readers trust *Gambling Times* to introduce powerful new winning strategies and systems. Using proven scientific methods, the world's leading experts show you how to win big money in the complex field of gambling.

Gambling Times has shown how progressive slot machines can be beat. Readers have discovered important new edges in blackjack. They've been shown how to know for sure when an opponent is bluffing at poker. *Gambling Times* has also spelled out winning methods for football, baseball and basketball. They've published profound new ways of beating horses. Their team of experts will uncover information in the months ahead that's certain to be worth thousands of dollars to you.

In fact, the features are so revolutionary that they must take special precautions to make sure *Gambling Times* readers learn these secrets long before anyone else. So how much is *Gambling Times* worth to you? Well...

NOW *GAMBLING TIMES* CAN BE BETTER THAN FREE! Here's how: This BONUS package comes AUTOMATICALLY TO YOU WHEN YOU SUBSCRIBE...or goes to a friend if you give a gift subscription.

(1) POKER BONUS at the TROPICANA card room in Las Vegas. Play poker at the TROPICANA and receive a free dinner buffet and comps to the "Folies Bergere" show for you *and* a guest. Value exceeds $40 excluding gratuities.

(2) FREE SPORTS BET. CHURCHILL DOWNS SPORTS BOOK in Las Vegas will let you make one wager up to $300 with no "vigorish." This means instead of laying the usual 11-to-10 odds, you can actually bet even up! You can easily save $30 here.

(3) PAYOFF BIGGER THAN THE TRACK. LEROY'S RACE BOOK, in Las Vegas, will add 10% to your payoff (up to $30 extra) on a special bet. Just pick the horse and the race of your choice, anywhere in America. For the first time in history, you can win more than the track pays.

(4) OUTSTANDING ROOM DISCOUNTS available only to *Gambling Times* subscribers. Check in at the SANDS in Las Vegas or Atlantic City, the TROPICANA in Atlantic City, the HIGH SIERRA in Lake Tahoe, or the CONDADO INN & CASINO in San Juan, Puerto Rico. Stay for 3 days and 2 nights and you'll save $29 off their normal low rates.

THAT'S A SAVING GREATER THAN THE ENTIRE COST OF YOUR SUBSCRIPTION.

USE ALL FOUR CERTIFICATES (VALID FOR ONE YEAR)...GET *GAMBLING TIMES* FREE...AND YOU'LL PUT $93 IN YOUR POCKET!

To begin your delivery of *Gambling Times* magazine at once, enclose a payment of $36.00 by check or money order (U.S. currency), Master-Card or Visa. Add $5.00 per year for postage outside the United States. Send payment to:

GAMBLING TIMES MAGAZINE
1018 N. Cole Avenue
Hollywood, California 90038

GAMBLING TIMES
MONEY BACK GUARANTEE

If at any time you decide *Gambling Times* is not for you, you will receive a full refund on all unmailed copies. You are under no obligation and may keep the bonus as a gift.

Other Valuable Sources of Knowledge Available Through *Gambling Times*

(See ordering information on page 188.)

Here are some additional sources you can turn to for worthwhile gambling information:

The Experts Sports Handicapping Newsletter.
Published monthly, this newsletter will show you how to become an Expert handicapper. You will learn the different styles of handicapping and be able to select the one method best suited to your personality. Yearly subscriptions are $60; $50 for *Gambling Times* subscribers.

The Experts Blackjack Newsletter.
This monthly newsletter has all the top blackjack Experts working just for you. Features answers, strategies and insights that were never before possible. Yearly subscriptions are $60; $50 for *Gambling Times* subscribers.

Poker Player.
Published every other week, this *Gambling Times* newspaper features the best writers and theorists on the poker scene today. You will learn all aspects of poker, from odds to psychology, as well as how to play in no-limit competition and in tournaments. Yearly subscriptions (26 issues) are $20.

Casino Marketing International.
CMI sponsors the largest prize-pool blackjack tournaments in the world. Using an exciting non-elimination format, CMI offers the tournament blackjack player the opportunity to play in each round of the tournament. In 1984 the Desert Inn in Las Vegas hosted the Blackjack Tournaments. In 1985 CMI expects to offer Blackjack Tournaments in Atlantic City and Reno/Lake Tahoe. For information on where and when the next tournaments will be held, write CMI, 8462 Sunset Boulevard, Penthouse Suite, Los Angeles, CA 90069, or call toll free (800) 421-4442. In California call (800) 252-7772.

Super/System: A Course in Power Poker by Doyle Brunson.
The bible for poker players. This book contains contributions from
poker's leading professionals, including Bobby Baldwin, Mike Caro
and David Sklansky. An encyclopedia of more than 600 pages of
detailed strategy for every form of poker.
Hardbound. $50.00. (Total shipping charges: $2.50).

OTHER BOOKS AVAILABLE

If you can't find the following books at your local bookstore, they may be
ordered directly from *Gambling Times,* 1018 N. Cole Ave., Hollywood, CA
90038. Information on how to order is on page 188.

Poker Books

According to Doyle by Doyle Brunson—Acknowledged by most people as
the world's best all-around poker player, twice World Champion Doyle
Brunson brings you his homespun wisdom from over 30 years as a professional poker player. This book will not only show you how to win
at poker, it will give you valuable insights into how to better handle that
poker game called LIFE.
Softbound. $6.95. (ISBN: 0-89746-003-0)

Caro's Book of Tells by Mike Caro—The photographic body language of
poker. Approximately 150 photographs with text explaining when a
player is bluffing, when he's got the winning hand—and WHY. Based
on accurate investigation; it is NOT guesswork. Even the greatest of
gamblers has some giveaway behavior. For the first time in print, one
of the world's top poker players reveals how he virtually can read minds
because nearly every player has a "tell." Seal the leaks in your poker
game and empty your opponent's chip tray.
Hardbound. $20.00. (ISBN: 0-914314-04-1)

The Gambling Times Official Rules of Poker by Mike Caro—Settles home
poker arguments. Caro has written the revised rule book (including a
section on etiquette) for the Horseshoe Club in Gardena, California,
that may soon be adopted by other clubs and become the California standard. He is presently scheduling a meeting of poker room managers

at the Bingo Palace in Las Vegas. This should lead to the creation of a uniform book of rules for Nevada cardrooms. *The Gambling Times Official Rules of Poker* includes sections of the rules from public cardrooms, but mostly it is for home poker. The book is needed because there presently exists no true authority for settling Friday night poker disputes.

Softbound. $5.95. (ISBN: 0-89746-012-X)

Poker for Women by Mike Caro—How women can take advantage of the special male-female ego wars at the poker table and win. This book also has non-poker everyday value for women. Men can be destroyed at the poker table by coy, cunning or aggressive women. That's because, on a subconscious level, men expect women to act traditionally. This book tells women when to flirt, when to be tough and when to whimper. Many of the tactics are tried and proven by Caro's own students. This book does not claim that women are better players, merely that there are strategies available to them that are not available to their male opponents.

Softbound. $5.95. (ISBN: 0-89746-009-X)

Poker Without Cards by Mike Caro—Applying world-class poker tactics to everyday life. Is the salesman bluffing? Can you get a better price? Negotiating is like playing a poker hand. Although poker tactics are common in daily encounters, few people realize when a hand is being played. It's hard to make the right decision when you're not even aware that you've been raised. The book is honest and accurate in its evaluation of behavior.

Softbound. $6.95. (ISBN: 0-89746-038-3)

Wins, Places, and Pros by Tex Sheahan—With more than 50 years of experience as a professional poker player and cardroom manager/tournament director, Tex lets his readers in on the secrets that separate the men from the boys at the poker table. Descriptions of poker events, playing experiences from all over the world, and those special personalities who are the masters of the game. . .Tex knows them all and lays it out in his marvelous easy-to-read style.

Softbound. $6.95. (ISBN: 0-89746-008-1)

Blackjack Books

The Beginner's Guide to Winning Blackjack by Stanley Roberts—The world's leading blackjack writer shows beginners to the game how to obtain an instant advantage through the simplest of techniques. Covering Basic Strategy for all major casino areas from Las Vegas to the Bahamas, Atlantic City and Reno/Tahoe, Roberts provides a simple system to immediately know when the remaining cards favor the player. The entire method can be learned in less than two hours and taken to the casinos to produce sure profits.
Softbound. $10.00. (ISBN: 0-89746-014-6)

The Gambling Times Guide to Blackjack by Stanley Roberts with Edward O. Thorp, Ken Uston, Lance Humble, Arnold Snyder, Julian Braun, Richard Canfield and other experts in this field—The top blackjack authorities have been brought together for the first time to bring to the reader the ins and outs of the game of blackjack. All aspects of the game are discussed. Winning techniques are presented for beginners and casual players.
Softbound. $5.95. (ISBN: 0-89746-015-4)

Million Dollar Blackjack by Ken Uston—Every blackjack enthusiast or gaming traveler who fancies himself a "21" player can improve his game with this explosive bestseller. Ken Uston shows you how he and his team won over 4 million dollars at blackjack. Now, for the first time, you can find out how he did it and how his system can help you. Includes playing and betting strategies; winning secrets, protection from cheaters, Uston's Advanced Point Count System, and a glossary of inside terms used by professionals.
Hardbound. $18.95. (ISBN: 0-914314-08-4)

Casino Games

The Gambling Times Guide to Casino Games by Len Miller—The co-founder and editor of *Gambling Times* magazine vividly describes the casino games and explains their rules and betting procedures. This easy-to-follow guide covers blackjack, craps, roulette, keno, video machines, progressive slots and more. After reading this book, you'll play like a pro!
Softbound. $5.95. (ISBN: 0-89746-017-0)

The Gambling Times Guide to Craps by N.B. Winkless, Jr.—The ultimate craps book for beginners and experts alike. It provides you with a program to tackle the house edge that can be used on a home computer. This text shows you which bets to avoid and tells you the difference between craps in Nevada and craps in other gaming resort areas. It includes a glossary of terms and a directory of dealer schools. Softbound. $5.95. (ISBN: 0-89746-013-8)

General Interest Books

According to Gambling Times: The Rules of Gambling Games by Stanley Roberts—At last you can finally settle all the arguments regarding what the rules are in every known gambling endeavor. From pari-mutuels to bookie slips, from blackjack to gin rummy, the rules of the games and the variations that are generally accepted in both public and private situations are clearly enumerated by the world's #1 gaming authority. Hardbound. $12.00. (ISBN: 0-914314-07-6)

The Gambling Times Guide to Gaming Around the World compiled by Arnold L. Abrams—The complete travel guide to legal gaming throughout the world. This comprehensive gaming guide lists casinos around the world; the games played in each; cardrooms and facilities; greyhound racing and horse racing tracks, as well as jai alai frontons, lotteries and sports betting facilities. This book is a must for the traveling gamer. Softbound. $5.95. (ISBN: 0-89746-020-0)

The Gambling Times Guide to Systems That Win, Volume I and Volume II—For those who want to broaden their gambling knowledge, this two-volume set offers complete gambling systems used by the experts. Learn their strategies and how to incorporate them into your gambling style. **Volume I** covers 12 systems that win for roulette, craps, backgammon, slot machines, horse racing, baseball, basketball and football. Softbound. $5.95. (ISBN: 0-89746-034-0)
Volume II features 12 more systems that win, covering horse racing, craps, blackjack, slot machines, jai alai and baseball. Softbound. $5.95. (ISBN: 0-89746-034-0)

The Gambling Times Guide to Winning Systems, Volume I and Volume II—For those who take their gambling seriously, *Gambling Times* presents a two-volume set of proven winning systems. Learn how the experts beat the house edge and become consistent winners. **Volume I** contains 12 complete strategies for casino games and sports wagering, including baccarat, blackjack, keno, basketball and harness handicapping.
Softbound. $5.95. (ISBN: 0-89746-032-4)
Volume II contains 12 more winning systems covering poker bluffing, pitching analysis, greyhound handicapping and roulette.
Softbound. $5.95. (ISBN: 0-89746-033-2)

Gambling Times Presents Winning Systems and Methods, Volume I and Volume II—This two-volume collection of winning strategies by some of the nation's leading experts on gambling will help you in your quest to beat the percentages. **Volume I** includes several chapters on black-jack, as well as methods for beating baseball, basketball, hockey, steeplechase and grass racing.
Softbound. $5.95. (ISBN: 0-89746-036-7)
Volume II contains an analysis of keno and video poker, as well as systems for success in sports betting and horse racing.
Softbound. $5.95. (ISBN: 0-89746-037-5)

The Mathematics of Gambling by Edward O. Thorp—The "Albert Einstein of gambling" presents his second book on the subject. His first book, *Beat The Dealer,* set the gambling world on its heels and struck fear into the cold-blooded hearts of Las Vegas casino-owners in 1962. Now, more than twenty years later, Dr. Thorp again challenges the odds by bringing out a simple to understand version of more than thirty years of exploration into all aspects of what separates winners from losers. . .knowing the real meaning of the parameters of the games.
Softbound. $7.95. (ISBN: 0-89746-019-7)

Odds: Quick and Simple by Mike Caro—How to know the right lines and win by figuring the odds logically. Common sense replaces mathematical formulas. This book will teach probabilities plainly and powerfully. The emphasis will be on gambling, showing how to quickly

determine whether or not to make a wager. Particular emphasis will be on sports bets, pot odds in poker, dice and various proposition bets. Also included will be tables of the most important gambling odds (craps, roulette, poker, blackjack, keno) for easy reference.
Softbound. $5.95. (ISBN: 0-89746-030-8)

P$yching Out Vegas by Marvin Karlins, Ph.D.—The dream merchants who build and operate gaming resorts subtly work on the casino patron to direct his attention, control his actions and turn his pockets inside out. At last, their techniques are revealed to you by a noted psychologist who shows you how you can successfully control your behavior and turn a losing attitude into a lifetime winning streak.
Hardbound. $12.00. (ISBN: 0-914314-03-3)

Winning by Computer by Dr. Donald Sullivan—Now, for the first time, the wonders of computer technology are harnessed for the gambler. Dr. Sullivan explains how to figure the odds and identify key factors in all forms of race and sports handicapping.
Softbound. $5.95. (ISBN: 0-89746-018-9)

Sports Betting Books

The Gambling Times Guide to Basketball Handicapping by Barbara Nathan—This easy-to-read, highly informative book is the definitive guide to basketball betting. Expert sports handicapper Barbara Nathan provides handicapping knowledge, insightful coverage, and step-by-step guidance for money management. The advantages and disadvantages of relying on sports services are also covered.
Softbound. $5.95. (ISBN: 0-89746-023-5)

The Gambling Times Guide to Football Handicapping by Bob McCune— Starting with the novice's approach to handicapping football, and winding up with some of the more sophisticated team selection techniques in the sports handicapping realm, this book will actually tell the reader how to forecast, *in advance,* the final scores of most major national football games. The author's background and expertise on the subject will put money into any sports gambler's pocket.
Softbound. $5.95. (ISBN: 0-89746-022-7)

The Gambling Times Guide to Greyhound Racing by William E. McBride—This complete discussion of greyhound racing is a must for anyone who is just beginning to appreciate this exciting and profitable sport. The book begins with a brief overview detailing the origins of greyhound racing and pari-mutuel betting, and explains the greyhound track environment, betting procedures, and handicapping methods. Includes an appendix of various greyhound organizations, a review of greyhound books, and an interesting section on famous dogs and personalities in the world of greyhound racing.
Softbound. $5.95. (ISBN: 0-89746-007-3)

The Gambling Times Guide to Harness Racing by Igor Kusyshyn, Ph.D., Al Stanley and Sam Dragich—Three of Canada's top harness handicapping authorities present their inside approach to analyzing the harness racing scene and selecting winners. All the important factors from the type of sulky, workouts, drivers' ratings, speed, pace, etc., are skillfully presented in simple terms that can be used by novices and experienced racegoers to find the likely winners.
Softbound. $5.95. (ISBN: 0-89746-002-2)

The Gambling Times Guide to Jai Alai by William R. Keevers—The most comprehensive book on jai alai available. Author Bill Keevers takes the reader on an informative journey from the ancient beginnings of the game to its current popularity. This easy-to-understand guide will show you the fine points of the game, how to improve your betting percentage, and where to find jai alai frontons.
Softbound. $5.95. (ISBN: 0-89746-010-3)

The Gambling Times Guide to Thoroughbred Racing by R.G. Denis—Newcomers to the racetrack and veterans alike will appreciate the informative description of the thoroughbred pari-mutuel activity supplied by this experienced racing authority. Activities at the track and available information are blended skillfully in this guide to selecting winners that pay off in big-ticket returns.
Softbound. $5.95. (ISBN: 0-89746-005-7)

UPCOMING *GAMBLING TIMES* BOOKS

The following books will be at your local bookstore by September, 1984. If you can't find them there, they may also be ordered directly from *Gambling Times*.

Poker Books

Caro's Poker Encyclopedia by Mike Caro—Features alphabetical definitions and discussions of poker terms. Extensively cross-indexed, it can be used as a reference book to look up important poker terms (ante, bluff, sandbag) or it can be pleasurably read straight through. The definitions are brief; the advice is in-depth.
Softbound. $8.95. (ISBN: 0-89746-039-1)

Free Money: How to Win in the Cardrooms of California by Michael Wiesenberg—Computer expert and poker writer par excellence, Michael Wiesenberg delivers critical knowledge to those who play in the poker rooms of the western states. Wiesenberg gives you the precise meaning of the rules as well as the mathematics of poker to aid public and private poker players alike. Wiesenberg, a prolific author, is published by more gaming periodicals than any other writer.
Softbound. $6.95. (ISBN: 0-89746-027-8)

The Railbird by Rex Jones—The ultimate kibitzer, the man who watches from the rail in the poker room, has unique insights into the character and performance of all poker players. From this vantage point, Rex Jones, Ph.D., blends his expertise and considerable education in anthropology with his lifetime of poker playing and watching. The result is a delightful book with exceptional values for those who want to avoid the fatal errors of bad players and capitalize upon the qualities that make up the winning strengths of outstanding poker players.
Softbound. $6.95. (ISBN: 0-89746-028-6)

Tales Out of Tulsa by Bobby Baldwin—Oklahoma-born Bobby Baldwin, the youngest player to ever win the World Championship of Poker, is considered to be among the top five poker players in the world. Known affectionately as "The Owl," this brilliant poker genius, wise beyond his years, brings the benefits of his experience to the pages of this book. It's sure to stop the leaks in your poker game, and you will be amazingly ahead of your opponents in the very next game you play.
Softbound. $6.95. (ISBN: 0-89746-006-5)

World Class Poker, Play by Play by Mike Caro—Once again, Caro brings the world of poker to life. This time he gives us a one-card-at-a-time analysis of world class poker, with many card illustrations. This book includes discussions of professional tactics, then simulates game situations and asks the reader to make decisions. Next, Caro provides the answer and the hand continues. This learn-while-you-pretend-to-play format is a favorite teaching method of Caro's and one which meets with a great deal of success.
Hardbound. $20.00. (ISBN: 0-914314-06-08)

General Interest Books

Caro on Computer Gambling by Mike Caro—Caro discusses computers and how they will change gambling. He provides winning systems and descriptions of actual programs. This book will give the novice a taste of how computers work. Using the Pascal programming language, Caro builds a working program step-by-step to show how a computer thinks and, also, how a human should analyze gambling propositions. This book is only slightly technical and mostly logical. Also discussed are ways that computers can cheat and speculation on the future of computers in gambling. Will you be able to type in your horse bets from your home computer? Can that personal computer be linked by phone into a perpetual poker game with the pots going straight into your bank account? The answers to these questions are found right here in Caro's book.
Softbound. $6.95. (ISBN: 0-89746-042-1)

The Gambling Times Quiz Book by Mike Caro—Learn while testing your knowledge. Caro's book includes questions and answers on the concepts and information published in previous issues of *Gambling Times*. Caro tells why an answer is correct and credit is given to the author whose *Gambling Times* article suggested the question. This book covers only established fact, not the personal opinions of authors, and Caro's inimitable style makes this an easy-reading, easy-learning book.
Softbound. $5.95. (ISBN: 0-89746-031-6)

How the Superstars Gamble by Ron Delpit—Follow the stars to the racetracks, ball games, casinos and private clubs. You'll be amazed at how involved these world famous personalities are in the gambling scene, and how clever they are at the games they play. Ron Delpit,

lifelong horse racing fan and confidant of innumerable showbiz greats, tells you fascinating tales about his friends, the superstars, with startling heretofore secret facts.
Hardbound. $12.00. (ISBN: 0-914314-17-3)

How to Win at Gaming Tournaments by Haven Earle Haley—Win your share of the millions of dollars and fabulous prizes being awarded to gaming contestants, and have the glory of being a World Champion. Poker, gin rummy, backgammon, craps, blackjack and baccarat are all popular tournament games. The rules, special tournament regulations, playing procedures, and how to obtain free entry are fully explained in this informative manual. The tournament promoters—who they are, where they hold events—and the cash and prizes awarded are explained in detail. Tournament play usually requires special strategy changes, which are detailed in this book.
Softbound. $8.95. (ISBN: 0-89746-016-2)

You're Comped: How to Be a Casino Guest by Len Miller—If you're a player you don't have to pay! Learn how to be "comped" in luxury casino-resort hotels the world over. A list of casinos together with names and addresses of junket representatives are included in this revealing guidebook. How to handle yourself on a junket is important if you want to receive all that you've been promised and be invited back again. How to do this, along with what you can expect from the casino, is explained in detail.
Softbound. $7.95. (ISBN: 0-89746-041-3)

Sports Betting Books

Fast Track to Harness Racing Profits by Mark Cramer——This systematic analysis of nuances in past performances will uncover patterns of improvement which will lead to flat bet profits. This book provides a functioning balance between creative handicapping and mechanical application.
Softbound. $6.95. (ISBN: 0-89746-026-X)

Fast Track to Thoroughbred Profits by Mark Cramer—A unique approach to selecting winners, with price in mind, by distinguishing between valuable and common-place information. Results: higher average pay-offs and solid flat bet profits. How to spot signs of improvement and when to cash in. And much, much more.
Softbound. $6.95. (ISBN: 0-89746-025-1)

Ordering Information

Send your book order along with your check or money order to:

Gambling Times
1018 N. Cole Ave.
Hollywood, CA 90038

Softbound Books: Please add $1.00 per book if delivered in the United States, $1.50 in Canada or Mexico, and $3.50 for foreign countries.

Hardbound Books: Shipping charges for the following books are $2.50 if delivered in the United States, $3.00 in Canada or Mexico, and $5.00 for foreign countries:

According to Gambling Times: The Rules of Gambling Games
Caro's Book of Tells
How the Superstars Gamble
Million Dollar Blackjack
P$yching Out Vegas
World Class Poker, Play by Play